Leadership Training for Softball

Using Mental Skills to Discover Your Potential

Aaron Weintraub

Cover and Text Illustrations by Josh Manges

Josh Manges prefers "illustrator" or "picture drawer" to "artist," which he says is far too pretentious. "Dad" is his favorite title. Between his house full of children and the corresponding hi-jinx, shenanigans, and tomfoolery, he claims it a wonder that anything gets done. He has a passion for both cartoons and comedy and since his household is chock-full of cartoon characters, he never has to go far for inspiration.

Note from the author: "Josh is an absolute joy to work with and is brilliant in his ability to take any and every idea, understand it, get the information he needs, and draw it beautifully."

© 2013 Aaron Weintraub. All rights reserved.
Printed in the United States by Signature Book Printing, www.sbpbooks.com

B.E.N. Press
5700 Alister Ln.
The Colony, TX 75056

Except as permitted under the United States Copyright Act of 1976, no part of this book may be reproduced, stored in a retrieval system, or transmitted, in any form or by any means, electronic, mechanical, photocopying, recording, or otherwise, without the prior written permission of the publisher.

ISBN: 978-0-9893227-0-6
Library of Congress Control Number: 2013909433

DEDICATION

to Ariel and Carissa

As you grow, I hope you like the information in this book because I know you will need superb leadership skills to overcome some genetic flaws.

ACKNOWLEDGMENTS

As an author, I am indebted to Dr. Bennett Weintraub, Bonnie Zarin, Shaun Dawson, Dr. Linda Bunker, Mike Fox, Fran Pirozzolo, Harvey Dorfman, Nicole Weintraub, and Nancy and Jason Weintraub. My Mom, Nancy, served as primary editor. As a coach, I would have no chance of being the writer that I am without the experiences and lessons learned from too many coaches and athletes to list. However, I would be remiss not to mention Dennis Womack, Kevin Shelton, Debbie Hedrick, Doug Kovash, Rusty Stroupe, Kevin Howard, Jeremy Farber, Mark Rueffert, Nate Rewers, Whitney Canion, Becca Collom, Paul Goldschmidt, Andy Jackson, Dave Keller, Carlos Tosca, John Boles, and of course Harvey Dorfman.

TABLE OF CONTENTS

Foreword by Mike Candrea xi
Preface xiii
It All Comes Down To One Pitch (Part 1) 1
Introduction – Don't Tell Me "Nice Try" 3

PART 1 – TOP JOCKS ARE SCIENTISTS

Chapter 1 – Control the Controllables 11
Chapter 2 – The Secret of Progress (Awareness) 17
    The Traffic Light Analogy 21
    All Lights Green (Gathering) 25
Chapter 3 – Smart Work Routs Hard Work 14-0 (Discipline) 29
Chapter 4 – Your Game, Your Zone (Peak Performance) 35
    Confident, Not Cocky 36
    To Care but Not Too Much 37

PART 2 – ATTITUDE, MEET ALTITUDE

Chapter 5 – She Wants It So Bad (Motivation) 43
    The Energizer Bunny (Relentlessness) 46
    Going Somewhere? (Mission) 48
Chapter 6 – Champions Look at it This Way (Perspective) 51
    Mistakes Are Good 54
    No Achievement Necessary?!? (Self-Worth) 58
Chapter 7 – Do Not Respect the Opponent... Respect the Game . . . 63
    Never Ass-u-me 65
Chapter 8 – Am I Talking To Myself? Am I Good at It? 67
    Yes is Best 73
    Common Patterns of Trudging Uphill into the Wind 75
    (Distorted or Irrational Self-Talk)
        Oh That Poor, Poor, Super-Talented Kid 75
        The Far From Perfect Perfectionist 77
        All or Nothing 78
        Never Say Never 79
        Can't Say Can't 79
        Hate the Word Hate 80
        There's No Crying in Softball (Catastrophizing) 81
        No Fair, No Kidding 82

It's All My Fault 82
Balanced Rationality is Bad 83
Excuses Are Sneaky 85
Frankly, I Do Give a Damn, but... 85
Running Downhill with the Wind (Transforming Self-Talk) 86
Chapter 9 – Building Swag 89
Good is Good; Bad is Good (Optimistic Explanatory Style) 91
Staying Unstuck on the Fast Track Up 95
Champions are Coachable 99
Dump the Slump 101
Put the Egg Before the Chicken (Confidence Precedes Greatness) . 103
Chapter 10 - Hyped to the Max (Controlling Performance Anxiety) 107
Acting Class 113
Body Language Speaks 115
Tight as a Drum, Loose as a Goose 116
Breathe or Die 118
Don't Just Win, Be Two Better 120
Chapter 11 – Achievements in Softball are Fun... and So Are Setbacks . . . 121

PART 3 – GET READY, GET SET

Chapter 12 – Begin with the End in Mind (Imagery) 127
Chapter 13 – I Will Not Be Denied (Preparation) 133
    Little is Big, Big is Little (Attention to Details) 135
    Becoming "Clutch" 137
    Illusions of Confidence or True Learning 140
Chapter 14 – Know Your Job to Do Your Job! 145
    Go Fast, Don't Crash 148
    No Doubt 150
Chapter 15 – Success... Guaranteed (Routines) 153
Chapter 16 – Instant Improvement (Anchoring) 159

PART 4 – GO! TIME

Chapter 17 – The Now 165
    Flush the "Poop" 168
    Don't Try Harder, Try Easier 170
Chapter 18 – Fine Focus 173
    Attend-WHAT? (Dimensions of Attentional Control) 177
Chapter 19 – Pressure: Yes, Collapse: No 179

Fear of Failure: Universal and Good 182
    Great Expectations 184
Chapter 20 – Execute! 185

PART 5 – NOW WHAT?

Chapter 21 - Accelerating Progress 189
    Use that Multi-Billion Neuron Brain 192
    Sorry is a No-No! 195
    The Snowball of Destruction 196
Chapter 22 – SMARTer Goals 203
Chapter 23 – T.E.A.M. First 207
    Form Follows Function… or Dysfunction 211
    Leaders Inspire Confidence 213

It All Comes Down To One Pitch (Part 2) 219

Appendix A – Reflective Worksheet 221
Appendix B – Traffic Light Analogy 222
Appendix C – Eight Mental Skills of Great Athletes Awareness Exercise . 223
Appendix D – Leadership Evaluation with 360° Feedback 226
Appendix E – Values Exercise 228
Appendix F – Positive Emotional Flood Exercise 232
Appendix G – Routines for a Specific Game Situation 234
Appendix H – Pre-Game Routine 235
Appendix I – Gathering Routine 236
Appendix J – Stop the Day, Start the Game 237
Appendix K – Goal Setting Worksheet #1 239
Appendix L – Short-Term Goal Tracking 240
Appendix M – Daily and Weekly Goal Log 241

References and Suggested Reading 243
About the Author 246

FOREWORD

I have had the honor to coach for the past 37 years at the junior college and Division I levels. The past 28 years I have been at the University of Arizona and have had the opportunity to watch our game grow in leaps and bounds. As I began my career, the game was dominated by pitching. We pitched from 40 feet and used a white ball with white seams and an aluminum bat. Since then, we have moved the mound back to 43 feet, used an optic yellow ball with red seams, and a composite bat that has heightened the performance of hitters today. The one constant in the game is the ability of our greatest performers to have a quiet mind and strong mental skills. Back in the day, these skills were severely overlooked and the knowledge and resources to help build them were hard to find. We all agreed that we played a game of relaxed skills, but how often did we give our athletes the tools and knowledge to play the game without distractions and to deal effectively with a game built around failure? I have constantly seen the greatest physically skilled athletes unable to perform at a high level and average players excel in our game due to their mental skill set.

I had the honor of coaching our 2004 and 2008 Olympic softball teams and probably witnessed one of the greatest performances by any team in Olympic history in Athens in 2004. This was a team of our very best softball players in the world and the common thread that I found in these players was their emotional stability and quiet minds. This team full of leaders had outstanding physical skills, but their ability to perform consistently under pressure was directly related to their ability to play the game one pitch at a time, embracing the opportunity to perform on the biggest stage. There are many distractions that come with the game, but these girls knew how to block them out. In today's athletic arena, it is a must for any coach to have an understanding of the distractions that enter our athlete's performance on a daily basis. We would all agree that everyone has potential to perform, but to actually do it, we must eliminate the interference – tension and distractions!

Aaron Weintraub has done a remarkable job in this book to give coaches and athletes a wealth of knowledge and tools to both discover and help others discover their mental skills. This book will improve your ability to lead and perform without distractions, once again having fun working at and playing this game with your teammates. I have found that the most important step is being aware of those negative thoughts, tension, and the fears that performing can bring, and then finding simple solutions to overcome the negative chatter in our mind that keeps us from a fluid performance motion. In the pages that follow, Aaron provides the details and tools to develop this awareness and proven strategies that work for the greatest athletes in the world. His style is impressive because it is in-depth and sophisticated while remaining easy to read and understand.

This book will not only help you perform in softball, but more importantly it will guide you to tap into your leadership skills that will help you reach your full potential in life! I love it when I have a team full of leaders and I am looking forward to giving each member of my team a copy of this book!

Mike Candrea

PREFACE

> Whatever you can do, or dream you can, begin it. Boldness has genius, power, and magic in it. Begin it now.
> —Johann Wolfgang von Goethe, Poet

> Success is the peace of mind that comes from knowing you did your best.
> —John Wooden, Basketball Hall of Famer as both a Player and Coach

Leadership is simultaneously common and elusive. Everyone talks about it. The need for it is omnipresent. The desire to be a leader is almost universal, yet effective leaders are rare. In short, leadership is easy to talk about and difficult to achieve.

At the risk of giving away the golden ticket before this book officially begins, leadership is a simple four-step process:

1. Have a clear vision
2. Lead by example
3. Connect with empathy, and
4. Have the resources left in the tank to help others to give their best effort, too.

This is not a step-by-step process, but rather a constant pursuit of all four elements. It cannot be achieved without interminable, subtle adjustments. Deficiency at any step in the process terminates the potential leader's effectiveness, sometimes permanently. The most common misstep is leading by example. The others are not easy, but they do not require as much courage and relentlessness as giving your best effort one step at a time, accepting whatever happens, and then doing it again.

Many athletes today want to lead and are willing to work, but they lack the mental toughness that equals the consistency of a leader. When you achieve consistent excellence, others will want to follow. This book provides the details for how to discover and display your potential, setting you up to be the ultimate competitor and leader. It is about leading others by first leading yourself effectively through the inevitable trials and tribulations of elite level sports. In the course of clarifying how to achieve this, it also provides the means to develop a clear vision, empathize with others, and have the positive energy and courage required to support others, too.

Many smart athletes believe that all it takes to win is talent and hard work, but experience teaches us that:

$$\text{Talent} + \text{Hard Work} \neq \text{Performance.}$$

Why do athletes perform well at certain times but poorly at others? Why do many work hard and have talent, but still fail to consistently get the results that they expect and deserve? Are they practicing efficiently? Do they know exactly what to do to guarantee a successful performance in "clutch" situations? The solutions exist not in athletes' physical skills or abilities, but in their mental skills. This book will guide an athlete or coach who wants to learn how to bridge the gap between potential and performance and consistently give best effort performances. Athletes must be clear about what they want to do, develop their self-awareness, and anchor successful thoughts, feelings, and behaviors. This book discusses leadership in fastpitch softball, though mental skills training breeds leaders in any performance situation.

Mental skills training significantly improves both rate of learning and performance under pressure. As the level of play increases, the impact of the mental side of the game increases, in large part because the differences in athletes' physical skills diminish. The physical mechanics of sports are often taught with impressive skill, but softball is typically a sink-or-swim world when it comes to mental skills. This is odd since mental toughness is the mark of every great leader. However, it is also good news because it means that you can get an edge over your competition by practicing mental toughness skills.

Most coaches know that attitude, focus, teamwork, self-control, confidence, courage, and other mental skills are the keys to great leadership, great execution, and great times on the diamond. Still, many do not dedicate much time to teaching these skills. Some coaches teach them haphazardly and some figure that the cream naturally rises to the top. It is not uncommon to hear a coach request (or demand) confidence and focus, but it is unusual for them to tell their athletes how to achieve these skills.

The top coaches in the country get their leadership edge through the four steps of leadership listed above. They have a clear vision about where their team is headed and how they will get there. They lead by example, because confidence, poise, focus, courage, and tenacity are required of them every bit as much as they are required of great athletes. They connect with empathy because they know that the majority of players do not care how much they know until they know how much they care. Finally, they have the resources to help their players give their best effort. They are not overwhelmed by the busy-ness of their jobs; they make time for what is important, including guidance for improving mental skills. When athletes are well trained in mental skills, they are able to coach themselves effectively and get better, faster.

Many coachable, hard-working athletes consistently perform far below their potential because they are unaware of their deficient mental skills. They hear comments like, "If we could just turn her brain off, she would be one heck of a player," but they have no strategies for keeping thoughts out of the way. They know that focus is desirable, but they have no clue about how to get locked in. Professional and Olympic athletes have formal mental skills training readily available. Now you do, too.

The lucky athletes are the ones who have parents and coaches who teach leadership skills effectively, usually without using labels like "sport psychology" and "mental skills training." (John Wooden is a great example.) Some universities now have a sport psychologist on staff or an undergraduate course related to coaching the mental game. This is progress, but there is still a long way to go. Poor coaching suggestions such as "RELAX," "We need…," or "Don't… [make this mistake]" are commonplace. Many coaches' personalities make it harder rather than easier for athletes to maintain an ideal attitude and focus.

I wrote this book because I want to help coaches and athletes increase the enjoyment they get from their investment in athletics. I want to accelerate the process of approaching potential for those with the courage and motivation to be uncomfortable, honest (synonym: aware), and persistent. I want to help athletes give their best efforts! You are an impressive person if you are really trying to approach your potential; most people prefer a safety net for their ego. I am honored if you find that my words aid your journey.

Sport psychology and leadership training may seem confusing and complex. They should not. This book will open up the world of mental skills training to you in an easy-to-understand manner. The principles are straightforward and logical, so if athletes can combine desire with discipline, acquiring these skills is inevitable. This book will guide that quest with clear definitions, common examples, relevant quotes, challenging ideas, intriguing stories, clarifying figures, action steps, and written exercises.

I began thinking of this book while in college in the early 1990s and began to actually write it in graduate school in the late 1990s. Many revisions followed. I love the question "Why?" "Why did that individual or team win?" Focusing on what is controllable, these questions follow:

- Why did that team or individual perform at that level in that situation?
- Why does one person break down under pressure while another breaks through?
- Why does the athlete who played so well one day play so poorly on another?

After a good deal of research, thought, trial-and-error with student-athletes, discussions with experts, and participation as an athlete or coach in well over 1,000 varsity contests, I have a fairly good understanding of how the combination of an athlete's mental and physical skills leads to her performances, which in turn leads to outcomes such as scoring and winning. This book is designed to share that understanding with you. It will also provide strategies to develop leadership skills so that an athlete's outcomes can most likely be the ones that she has always dreamed of.

The course of study herein is a progressive one divided into five parts. Part 1 (Top Jocks are Scientists) discusses the foundation skills of control, awareness, and discipline. Part 2 (Attitude, Meet Altitude) discusses how to optimize attitude, including confidence, for performance. Part 3 (Get Ready, Get Set) discusses the skills needed to have the best approach possible. Part 4 (Go!) looks at what to do when it is time to perform (preview: focus and trust your stuff). Finally, Part 5 (Now What?) addresses responses, thus completing the performance cycle. Responses include responding effectively to both situations and other people. Effective responses lead to effective approaches, and then a quality approach and a "locked-in" focus lead to superior performances. These behaviors combined with a proper attitude throughout will guarantee success as it is defined in these pages. They will *also* ensure the best possible chance of achieving all the positive outcomes that typically define success.

Sport psychology has been called the study of what successful athletes do. I am a quote fan, and I have included many sport psychology quotes that relate to the topic being discussed. These quotes demonstrate that many famous athletes have superb mental skills. Any athlete can own these skills if she has enough desire, patience, and persistence. Be pleased with small steps; developing mental skills is a process like any other. It takes time and effort. Athletes must take it one step at a time, for if they continuously make appropriate adjustments, they will continually improve. Occasional leaps forward in performance are likely, but no shortcuts exist. Continual improvement, itself, is the essence of success.

Before you begin, I am tempted to wish you luck in your pursuit of excellence. But since one point of all that follows is to take luck out of the equation as much as possible, I will resist. Instead, I wish you personal excellence and growth as you figure out more and more details about how to coach yourself and others towards peak performances. And I trust that because you are sincere in your motivations, disciplined in your approach, and courageous enough to know that your best effort is always good enough, the outcomes will work out for you just fine.

IT ALL COMES DOWN TO ONE PITCH (PART 1)

> Nobody who ever gave their best effort regretted it.
> —George Halas, Athlete, Coach, and Owner

It is the bottom of the seventh inning in the last game of the Super Regionals. A record crowd is on hand and fired up to watch two powerhouse teams duke it out in pure championship competition. It is "put up" or "shut up" time, because this will be the final game of the year for the loser, but the catapult to the College World Series for the winner. The first two games have been close, but this final game is the best one yet. In the bottom of the second inning, Ashley's team opened the scoring with a single run on a beautiful triple off the center field wall, but the visitors answered with a two-run home run in the top of the fifth. Since then, the pitching has dominated, keeping the score at 2-1. Now it is the bottom of the seventh, there are runners on first and third, two outs, and one of the best hitters in the country is up to bat. It is "Do or Die" time. Ashley is on deck.

Ashley truly loves softball; her life has revolved around the game for the past 15 years. She is a senior who has had a solid collegiate career. She will probably not get a chance to play professional softball, however, because she stands only 5'2" tall and there are so few available jobs. The possibility that this will be her last game playing organized ball briefly crosses her mind as the count on the current batter goes to 3-2. In the stands, the fans love this excitement. Despite their confidence in the home team, which has already won 45 games this year, many hearts are pounding as though they are trying to escape from their cages. In the dugout and in the stands, palms are sweaty and stomach butterflies are jumping. Through the incredible tension of this moment, the pitcher throws a nasty rise ball... and the batter lays off of it. It is too high... ball four.

Now, Ashley must step into the batter's box.

Is she ready? Is she sufficiently prepared to not just try hard, but to actually give her best effort?

(At the book's conclusion, you will find out more about Ashley and what happened next in "It All Comes Down to One Pitch: Part 2.")

INTRODUCTION

Don't Tell Me "Nice Try"

"Mental toughness is many things and rather difficult to explain. Its qualities are sacrifice and self-denial. Also, most importantly, it is combined with a perfectly disciplined will that refuses to give in. It's a state of mind – you could call it character in action."
—Vince Lombardi, Football Coach

Developing and refining my mental game has played a critical role in my success. For years, players have had to develop these skills on their own.
—Dave Winfield, Baseball Hall of Famer

Solid training in the mental game allows us to meet obstacles head-on and play with every ounce of our ability.
—Jim Abbott, (one-handed) Baseball Player

"Leaders are made, they are not born. They are made by hard effort, which is the price which all of us must pay to achieve any goal that is worthwhile."
—Vince Lombardi, Football Coach

"Nice try."

It sounds like a compliment, but is it? Close only counts in horseshoes. No one says "nice try" after a best effort performance. They say, "Wow!" "Awesome!" or "You did it!"

After the game, if someone asks if a player or team tried hard, the answer would consistently be "yes." But was it truly their best effort? Probably not, because tapping into the personal power necessary to perform the best they are capable of at that moment in time requires a lot more than trying hard. Trying is a huge part of it, and the motivation to compete with consistent intensity is not something to take for granted. However, to give a best effort performance, athletes also have to create an ideal performance state, commit to their plan, and focus completely on the task at hand.

Implementing the leadership skills discussed in this book will literally guarantee that an athlete knows how -- and is able -- to give her best effort for each and every performance. It is a lofty goal… and achieving it is completely within every athlete's control. Unfortunately, most athletes will fall far short of this goal because doing so will require patterns of thoughts and actions that are neither normal nor natural. On second thought, perhaps this is not so unfortunate because a willingness to understand and do what it takes to give best performances will give leaders an edge over their competition.

A common misconception in the sports world is that if a person practices and trains hard enough physically, everything else will magically fall into place. Reality frequently teaches otherwise. Mountains of both anecdotal and academic evidence exist that support the idea that mental skills are critical for an athlete to perform up to her potential. A web search for the keywords "sport psychology" will reveal millions of links. Over 95 percent of American Olympians in the past 45 years have received formal mental skills training. Today, sport psychologists or mental skills coaches are employed by almost every NFL, MLB, NBA, and NHL team, by most of the world's top professional golfers and tennis players, by IMG Academies, and even by some of the more progressive sports agents.

Mental toughness is the ability to do what needs to be done right now. Mentally tough competitors get more satisfaction from their time at practice and in competition than others because they know how to enjoy the game and its challenges. They have faith in the process that leads to great outcomes, so they do not worry about outcomes as much as most competitors do. Their consistency makes them a coach's favorite and somebody their teammates can rely on. They are leaders who always find a way to give their team a chance to win.

Leaders have the courage to do what is difficult and the confidence to be comfortable in a situation that would make others uncomfortable. They do not allow themselves to get frustrated because they will not accept the major ups and downs that most (overly emotional) athletes have. They find a way to keep their mind and body close to their ideal performance state. They find a way to do their job!

So how does an athlete acquire mental toughness? Can a leader be built? Athletes must know their job to do their job and no one is born with all the details. They must look for answers from many sources, then also be willing to guess so they can find out what works for themselves. Every time an athlete takes action with positive expectations (even through the inevitable adversities) and gives her best effort, she is practicing her mental skills and improving her mental toughness.

There are no shortcuts. However, there are many tools to help athletes accelerate the process of reaching their goals. The word "opportunity" is one example. Listen to the top professional athletes in interviews after they did well and you will find this theme: they were grateful for and thriving on the opportunities they had.

How mentally tough is each athlete? Does she know how to imitate the thought patterns of the greatest athletes in the world? Does she know how to move beyond normal, move beyond trying hard, to consistently giving her best effort? If she is going to get rewards from softball that most others will not get, she will have to do things that most others are simply not willing to do! (For example, most will not read this book and even fewer will do what it suggests, even though they will not doubt the efficacy of what follows.)

Performance comes from the combination of physicals skills and mental skills. Physical skills include speed, strength, genetics, and mechanics. Mental skills is an umbrella term that includes everything else that affects performance such as attitude, focus, courage, teamwork, strategy, imagery, and confidence. How important is the mental side of the game? Most professional athletes say it is at least 80% of the equation. Whatever the number, athletes all recognize that the ability to deal with "failure," be in the moment, and trust their stuff is a difference maker. An important question follows: how much time do most athletes spend… how much of their attention in training is dedicated to improving their mental skills?

> **"You can either find a way or you can find an excuse, but you can't do both."**

Normal athletes spend most of their time thinking about mechanics and training physically. They miss out on many opportunities to train their mental game. Perhaps this is because they have not been exposed to the details about how to do it. Leaders recognize that mental skills is important and often under-coached, so they take the bull by the horns to find out how to get what they want. After all, they invest lots into softball and it is superb mental skills that will enable them to maximize their return on that investment. They know that by looking hard enough for the answers, they will find them. Quite a few are included in the pages that follow, but potential leaders be forewarned: knowing what to do is much easier than doing it.

Athletes improve their mental skills when they work smart. Many girls practice their drills, run their sprints, and lift weights. Very few people are willing to pay attention to the details so they can figure out more about themselves and more about the game. Even fewer will do what it takes to apply everything they learn. Doing so is tough, but this is great news for leaders, because this allows them to get an edge by being willing to do what others will not do! This book will help illuminate the path that leaders are already on, putting the wind at their backs. The primary goal herein is to approach potential by getting better, faster.

Even though it is obvious, an important principle to remember is that, "All you can do is all you can do" or "All you can control is all you can control." Athletes cannot control other people, the weather, or the past. Getting upset about a mistake by self, teammate, or umpire is normal, but it is not useful. Athletes can control themselves, including how they respond to challenges, what attitude they practice and perform with, and how fast they learn. Are they learning to be relaxed, confident, ready to go, committed to the plan, and focused one play at a time? They can be if they will think like a scientist does by experimenting for answers and making learning more important than today's results. They can leave normal far in the distance behind by making it a habit to give their best effort one step at a time.

Figure I-1

Rate of learning is critical. Every opportunity on the diamond can teach an athlete more about what works and what does not. Because a leader is mentally tough, she is not merely going through the required motions, she is practicing her physical and mental skills, testing her hypotheses, and paying attention to the results. Obviously learning more means that over time, she will win more than others. Her consistent hard and smart work through all the adversities of life (er... softball) is her edge. She stays relentless in her pursuit of excellence by doing common things like hitting, running, catching, and throwing in uncommon ways. She knows how to enjoy her job and do her job!

Both physical skills training and mental skills training are necessary to approach potential in any performance situation, and a clear understanding about how to train both is a large part of the battle. This book will help athletes to effectively coach themselves and others to approach potential. Athletes working hard on their mental game will gain awareness of what to look for and what to avoid. By understanding how thoughts impact performances, they will know how to practice smart. By having the courage to do their best at implementing what they know, they will find that the grind of championship pursuits becomes gradually easier. Great habits free up their internal resources, allowing them to focus more on how to help others effectively. Mentally tough competitors become leaders both on and off the field.

Two broad purposes exist for improving mental skills: performance enhancement and personal growth. Fortunately, the requirements for both are the same. Without guidance, acquisition of these mental skills is haphazard and slow. Systematic improvement to an athlete's mental game can clearly provide an edge over her unguided competition. Athletes who are in a hurry to find out how good they can become will be attracted to this course of study.

Leaders do not accept the idea that getting "hot" is something that merely happens by chance. It is true that an athlete cannot make it happen, but she can increase the frequency that it happens and its duration. She must accept responsibility for coaching herself towards her best possible performance by putting herself in a position to succeed. She must learn to control the controllables to perform up to her potential. What can she control? Here are some details…

PART 1

TOP JOCKS ARE SCIENTISTS

There is a choice you have to make,
In everything you do.
So keep in mind that in the end,
The choice you make, makes you.

Scientists have goals and race for progress. So do top athletes. Scientists form hypotheses about what will work and design experiments to test their ideas. So do top athletes. When something works, scientists are excited and plan to do it again. So do top athletes. And when an experiment "fails," scientists are still pleased because they use that information to make effective adjustments. Most athletes are not pleased when their experiment does not work. Their attitude about striking out is the opposite of positive.

Leaders are relentlessly positive. "Every wrong attempt discarded is another step forward," said Thomas Edison. By learning what works and what does not, scientists achieve progress. They do not have the emotional ups and downs that are so typical in athletics because the word "failure" is not in their vocabulary. The greatest athletes in the world share a common goal: to be the best they can be. They deal effectively with the challenges inherent to sport and competition by thinking like a scientist. They consistently make learning more important than the result of any single experiment.

Before the specifics of ideal practice and performance behaviors are discussed in Parts 2-5, a thorough understanding of the foundation of an athlete's mental game is needed. This foundation is built on controllable skills, including awareness of where she is and where she wants to be in any category or situation. It also includes her discipline, which provides the means to acquire skills, both physical and mental.

Leaders do not lead sometimes, they lead all the time. This is achieved through habits, including the habits of competitiveness, self-control, alertness, discipline, and confidence. They are not perfect at these, but they try to be. With knowledge (including what is found in the pages that follow) and the motivation and courage to take massive action based on that knowledge, consistency is achieved.

CHAPTER 1

CONTROL THE CONTROLLABLES

> I pray not for victory, but to do my best.
> —Amos Alonzo Stagg, Football Coach

> I've brainwashed myself to remember that you can't control your last pitch. It's already been thrown, so get over it. All you can control is the next pitch you're going to throw.
> —Kevin Brown, Baseball Pitcher

> It's easy to say success is having a gold medal or winning a championship, but I think it is much more than that. It's being able to know I did absolutely everything I could possibly do to win. The results are less significant than the effort.
> —Kelly Williams, 1998 Female Athlete of the Year, U.S. Fencing Association

> I can control the pitches I make, how I handle my mechanics, how I control my frame of mind. [It] benefited me most… when I realized that I can't control what happens outside of my pitching.
> —Greg Maddux, Baseball Pitcher

> You have no control of what goes on around you, but you have total control of how you respond to what goes on around you.
> —Ken Ravizza, Sport Psychologist

Softball players should know what can be controlled and what cannot. Uncontrollable aspects of softball include genetics, the other team's performance, adjudication, and other aspects of luck. Even teammates' behavior and coaching decisions are outside of the athlete's control. Behavior, on the other hand, is completely controllable. Behavior includes all details of an athlete's attitude, approach, focus, and response (the next four major parts of this book). It also includes the mechanics of the athlete's performance, which is determined by a combination of mental skills and physical skills. All of an athlete's skills come from her (uncontrollable) genetic potential in any category and her (controllable) preparation.

Control is paramount. Clearly, trying to control uncontrollable variables will lead to frustration and disappointment. It makes no sense to be concerned with things that cannot be controlled, yet everyone falls into that trap at times. Any attempt by an athlete to have absolute control over outcomes is futile. She should not try to win the game; she should try to give her team the best chance possible to win the game. The difference is subtle, but huge. One is controllable; the other is not.

An athlete needs to know her job if she is going to do it effectively. Coaching advice about what to do can help significantly, but ultimately the athlete decides what she is trying to do. It is important that she learn to define her job appropriately. The answer to the question, "What am I trying to do on this play?" may have multiple 'if/then' statements, but ultimately her job should be defined in completely controllable terms. Trying to control too much can be a double-edged sword because it leads both to frustration and to neglect of what can be controlled, namely, behavior. John Wooden said, "Don't whine, don't complain, and don't make excuses." An athlete behaves like a champion by maintaining self-control and doing her best to execute her appropriately defined job in every situation.

Figure 1-1

Wooden is a coach who clearly understands the impact of thoughts on performance, and history proves that he taught his players to think effectively. Who is the greatest coach ever? It is impossible to say for sure, but the discussion must include John Wooden. According to him, he never spoke to his players about winning a basketball game. Nevertheless, his basketball teams at UCLA won 10 national championships over a 12-year period. At one point, they won 88 straight games. Wooden did speak often of what it takes to do your best. His Pyramid of Success (Figure 1-2) clarifies the steps necessary to climb to the pinnacle, which is success.

To help maintain control and focus attention appropriately, athletes and coaches should be meticulous with their choice of words. Both self-talk and spoken words will either facilitate or interfere with ideal feelings and behaviors. Most people use words nonchalantly, but clarity in communication is achieved with specific choices of words and specific definitions of those words. The following terms are used by the author in a specific manner to clarify controllability. *Outcomes* are results that include at least one uncontrollable variable, whereas *behavior* is always completely controllable. The common word *result* is often good to avoid; like behavior, it should be used only when all factors are controllable.

It is useful to avoid certain "bad" words in performance situations. This will be explored further in Chapter 8, but the Table 1-1 gives a summary of words that inhibit performance. Notice that it is always possible, though sometimes challenging, to express the same idea in terms that do not include these "bad" words.

Table 1-1[1]

Change these "curse" words…	to these good words
Can't	Can
I'm not	I am
Need/Have to/Gotta	Want to
Should/Supposed to	Could
Apologizing	No outward response; good adjustment
Fail	Part of the process
Always/Never	Usually / might
Slump	Overdue

Sometimes it is easier to notate the danger of a particular word than to avoid it completely. Quotation marks can often serve this purpose. They indicate that the word being used is not completely true, at least not in the way the word is most commonly used. This avoids undesirable self-fulfilling prophecies or negative attitudes. People know what is meant by words like "fail," "always," "slump," or "clutch," but the quote marks indicate that something about the words are false. A "failure" is really a stepping stone to success. "Need" to win is not a requirement for continued life. A "slump" is real only if the athlete believes in it; otherwise, it

---

[1] Examples and more details are posted online at:
www.CoachTraub.com/images/pdfs/GoodWordsandCurseWords.pdf

is just one of the inevitable performance declines in life. A "clutch" situation is *not* special because champions give their best effort on each and every play.

Figure 1-2: The Pyramid of Success by John R. Wooden

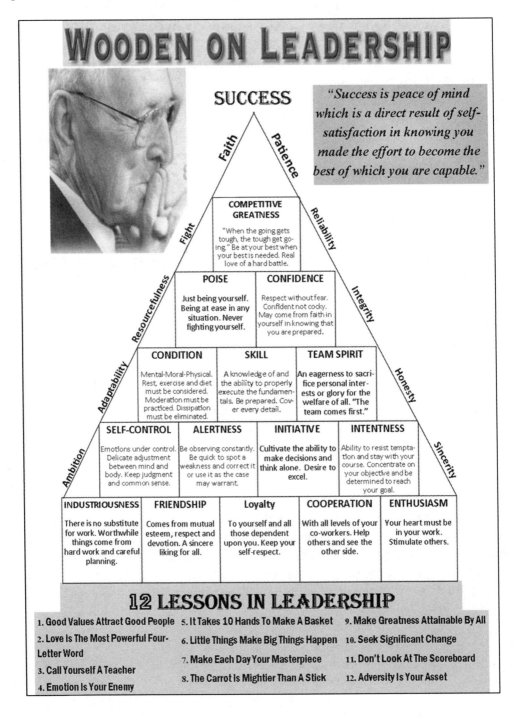

Success is an interesting word because beliefs about what defines success have a huge impact on the quality of an athlete's mental skills. John Wooden's definition is ideal: "The peace of mind that comes from knowing you did your best to become the best which you were capable of becoming." If an athlete earns this peace of mind, she is also doing everything she can to maximize her chances at getting success as most people define it: winning, awards, recognition, escape from embarrassment, etc.

To earn peace of mind means to have no regrets. To have no regrets, there has to be assurance about what a best effort really is. It is much more than simply trying hard. Mental skills training helps clarify what is necessary to give a best effort performance. In simplest terms, an athlete must try hard and achieve three goals to the best of her ability that day to give a best effort performance: create an ideal performance state, commit to her plan of attack, and focus.

America's competitive culture teaches that outcomes are important. Children almost always learn, incorrectly, to believe that if they do not win, then they are losers. Because of uncontrollable variables, it is possible for athletes to win on the scoreboard when they perform well below their potential or to lose when they perform close to their best. Although it is illogical to try to control things that cannot be controlled, outcomes usually become the object of concern for athletes and, unfortunately, for many people around these athletes. Many parents' first question after missing a game is, "Did you win?" "How many hits did you get?" Or, "What was the score?"

Figure 1-3

A healthy self-concept is based entirely on controllable issues and leads directly to improved performances. To fully succeed at "merely" trying to give herself the best chance possible to win, an athlete must believe that doing her best is more important than winning. It is simple to understand that all an athlete can do is all she can do, but it is tougher to embrace the idea that if she achieves this difficult goal of giving her best effort, but her team loses the game, she is a winner. Hopefully, the remainder of this book will help crystallize this challenging and critical concept: success is not winning. Success is doing your best.

John Wooden found this poem in a barbershop and it became one of his favorites:

> *At God's footstool to confess,*
> *A poor soul knelt and bowed his head.*
> *"I failed," he cried. Thy Master said,*
> *"Thou didst thy best, that is success."*

Following are some related ideas that Wooden liked to share:

- "Never try to be better than the next person, but never stop trying to be the best you can be."

- "Be more concerned with your character than your reputation. Your character is what you really are, while your reputation is merely what others think you are."

- "Success is not something that others can give to you."

Ideally, what others think of an athlete has little impact on what she thinks of herself. She may want to use their opinions to assist her dedication to reality, as their feedback may assist her search for what is real or correct and what is not. Clearly, though, the way she thinks of herself is most important. Doing her best becomes the only critical issue from which her self-evaluation is formed. This perspective frees the mind from worry about outcomes, allowing a complete focus on the task at hand. Since focus is a (perhaps the) critical component of performance, this mastery perspective actually leads to winning more than trying to win. Counterintuitive? Perhaps. True? Absolutely.

> This definition of success sounds familiar:
> **"Success is measured by your discipline and inner peace."**
> —Mike Ditka, Football Hall of Famer

Chapter 2

The Secret of Progress (Awareness)

Competition in its best form is a test of self. It has nothing to do with medals. The winner is the person who gets the most out of himself.
—Al Oerter, Four-Time Olympic Gold Medalist

You can learn more character on the two-yard line than anywhere else in life.
—Paul Dietzel, Football Coach, including 1958 NCAA Championship

The principle is competing against yourself. It's about self-improvement, about being better than you were the day before.
—Steve Young, Football Hall of Famer

Before an athlete can successfully execute a task to the best of her ability, she must know specifically what she is trying to do. What is required? She needs to set the stage for a peak performance by getting into an ideal state (of mind and body) and she needs to commit to an effective plan of attack. What mental skills does she lack? An athlete does not know what she does not know, so how can she know if her mental skills are strong or weak? These questions could discourage a timid person from training her mind. This would be a mistake because like gravity, mental skills will affect people whether they realize it or not. It would also be a mistake because all skills, physical and mental, improve with proper practice. The secret of progress is learning what works – the pursuit of awareness.

Mental skills are not mysterious or magical. It is not necessary to spend a decade meditating on a mountain in Tibet to learn how to focus. Rather, mental skills are logical concepts that enable an athlete to consistently bridge the gap between potential and performance. In learning how to approach their potential, leaders adopt the attitude of a scientist whose laboratory is herself. This single change in perspective, from discouragement and anger when outcomes are poor to a scientist's curiosity about what went wrong, can have wondrous effects.

Another way to think of mental skills is the set of all variables that affect performance other than genetic talent and physical skills. Physical and mental skills depend on each other and are usually trained simultaneously. Performing repetitions (e.g. taking fungoes, swinging, pitching) is physical practice. Performing repetitions with a specific objective in mind (e.g. fielding the ball out front, short swing to the hitting zone and long through it, or hitting spots aggressively) is physical and mental practice. The mental skills being practiced include concentration and mental toughness, which is simply the ability to do the job without regard to circumstance. Confidence and focus also increase with quality repetitions. To get the most benefit from practice, the athlete must work hard and smart, not just hard. (Coach Wooden used the word industriousness in his Pyramid of Success to represent this concept; it is one of the two cornerstones).

Following are some of the most important mental skills, or the variables other than physical skill and talent that affect performance:

- Adjustments
- Aggressiveness
- Approach
- Attitude
- Awareness
- Balance
- Commitment
- Communicativeness
- Competitiveness
- Confidence
- Consistency
- Continuous growth (Kaizen)
- Control
- Courage
- Discipline
- Enjoyment
- Faith
- Flexibility
- Focus
- Forgiveness
- Goal setting
- Handling failure
- Humility
- Imagery
- Intelligence
- Intensity
- Loyalty
- Meditation
- Mental toughness
- Patience
- Persistence
- Perspective
- Plan of attack
- Playing for yourself
- Poise
- Positivism
- Preparation
- Presentness
- Pride
- Relentlessness
- Resilience
- Respect
- Responses
- Self-esteem
- Self-talk
- Staying within yourself
- Teamwork
- Will / motivation / desire

Awareness is the foundation skill that all other mental skills are built on because *without awareness, no adjustment is possible*. Paying attention to life as it goes by and being conscientiously reflective enhance awareness. (Wooden called this building block of success *alertness*.) Reflection after performance is an oft-missed opportunity for athletes to increase awareness. The sooner the better, since memories fade with time. This reflection can be done formally with discussions, journaling, goals, and reflective worksheets[2] or informally by the athlete taking time specifically to think about what happened and what she would like to happen next time.

Figure 2-1

Other strategies exist for increasing awareness. Good coaches and teammates help bring awareness to instances when it is lacking by pointing out flaws (athletes with low self-esteem often resent this feedback, while athletes with high self-esteem welcome and even look for it). Meditation can also enhance recall of things that were temporarily lost inside the subconscious mind. Reviewing videotape of what actually happened can stimulate a huge leap in awareness. Whatever the strategy, it is critical to shun the response "I don't know." Claiming "I don't know" is taking the easy way out; it is what a majority of athletes do. Of course, it is difficult and unlikely to know exactly what went wrong, but that is no excuse not to try to know. Athletes with superior awareness make their best guess, then test this guess like any scientist would: with an experiment to see what works. With time and effort, they become skilled guessers.

Athletes can and should learn from history's great performers. Michael Jordan was perhaps the best basketball player ever. He had exceptional physical skills, but it was his superior mental skills that separated him from other very good basketball players. The following excerpts from his autobiography, *For the Love of the*

---

[2] See Appendix A – Reflective Worksheet

Game: My Story (1998), support this opinion (related mental skills are noted in brackets):

> *I listened, I was aware of my success, but I never stopped trying to get better. From my first day in the league to the last, I always felt I had a lot to prove. My expectations never changed. The better I got the better I wanted to become [Kaizen]. My appetite to learn was born out of my desire to... have as much control over the process as possible.*
>
> *I could see the fear in the eyes of other players, especially when they said something they weren't sure they could back up. Let's say someone swears he's going to play better the next night. But once the game starts that player misses her first shot. At that moment you can detect the slightest hesitation, the first hint of fear. Instead of looking at the situation and saying, 'OK, I have a good feel for the game now. I'll make the next one,' one negative starts building upon another [positive self-talk]. It's like they start building this wall, one negative piled upon another, until they have no chance of finding a way to knock it down. If I missed a shot, so what? I had the freedom to accept the consequence. I wasn't going to let a missed shot or a mistake affect the rest of my night [responses]. I never allowed the negatives to carry over and pile up. In those moments, I relied upon past experience. I'd go back to games where I missed my first five shots and then made the next ten [imagery]. I would try to bring that confidence into the moment [confidence]. By staying in the moment, I was never focused on what might happen two or three minutes later [presentness], which meant I wasn't thinking about the negative possibility of missing another shot [perspective, control]. Why would I worry about a shot I hadn't even taken yet? That kind of thinking limits everyone, not just athletes. They aren't comfortable with their skills and they don't have a good connection with their inner being [self-esteem]. I tried to improve each and every day. I needed to be able to look back to yesterday and feel like I'm better today. During the game it was a matter of keeping your poise, learning how to settle your nerves in the heat of the moment [control].*
>
> *If you practice the way you play, there shouldn't be any difference [discipline]. That's why I practiced so hard. I wanted to be prepared for the game. I practiced hard enough that the games were often easier. That's exactly what I was trying to achieve. No*

one can turn it on without preparing themselves in practice. ...I took pride in the way I practiced.

The Traffic Light Analogy

> Everybody has limits. You just have to learn what your own limits are
> and deal with them accordingly.
> —Nolan Ryan, Baseball Hall of Famer

Reflective exercises help athletes gain awareness of their own strengths and weaknesses. They may seem tedious, but they are important, since awareness is the foundation skill that enables appropriate adjustments. In the traffic light analogy, the athlete identifies signals within himself, and the results she is producing indicate that the stage is set to perform superbly (green light: "Go!"), fairly (yellow light: "Warning."), or poorly (red light: "Stop! Make it right.").

Of course, the goal for the softball player is to always have a "green light" when the pitch is delivered. This "green light" will sometimes happen by chance. When it fails to happen on its own, it is the athlete's responsibility to make it happen. She will only be able to create a "green light" when the following occurs:

- She knows her traffic light signals.
- She remembers to check her signals shortly before the performance begins.
- If something is wrong, she gathers herself to get back to her "green" "Go!" signal.

Before she can use the tools to change the light from "yellow" or "red" to "green" (gathering strategies), she must learn to recognize her personal signals.

A "green light" informs the athlete that she is in control of herself and in her ideal state for this performance. She has the right attitude and the right physiology (e.g., hype level control, muscle tension, and breathing patterns). The stage is set for a peak performance. Therefore, like the driver on the road who sees the green light, she should keep going, making no change in behavior. She is ready to commit to an effective plan of attack and then focus in on the task at hand. She is ready to give her best effort.

What are some common "green light" indicators? Certainly, good results (and outcomes) are great, easy-to-recognize indicators, especially if the athlete is trying to repeat the same task. However, knowing other indicators that are available before she performs is also useful. The most common of these indicators is an appropriate, confident attitude. What is appropriate? Whatever has worked best in the past. Usually, she is having fun and enthusiastic, determined, and aggressive under control. She is confident and knows exactly what to do. This attitude and relaxed breathing helps produce an ideal physiology, including an internal, relaxed state in which the action seems to be going nice and slow. Her hype level is just right, which might be a noticeable green light because it is indicated by her self-talk being calm rather than nervous or because her breathing is steady, deep, and easy.

Figure 2-2

Different people have different ideal attitudes. Also, the same person may perform one task well from one attitude and a different task well from a different attitude. One example of an ideal attitude is the need for an athlete to prove herself worthy of respect (major upsets often occur when the underdogs set out to prove themselves and the favorites are cocky and complacent). Another athlete may find that "relaxed enthusiasm" produces her best results. Perhaps more or less aggressiveness is their key factor. One athlete may need to be pumped up and motivated, while another athlete doing the same task needs to calm down, slow down, and let the game come to her. Many athletes define their ideal attitude as confident, relaxed or comfortable, energized, and having fun. It is each athlete's job to figure out what works best for her for each task and then do her best to create that ideal state for every performance. Finding and executing such a routine is a process that takes time and experience, so again, the *athlete as scientist exploring what works* is a useful analogy.

Another interesting example of an ideal state was reported by basketball star Reggie Miller, who said he needed to "feel the hate" for his opponent to play his best. Certainly, the aggressiveness this attitude generates is appropriate in competition and can be 100 percent distinct from a kind-hearted disposition outside of competition. However, if an athlete believes her ideal state is one which she has trouble getting to regularly or she needs factors outside her control to happen to get her there, she is wrong. Her ideal state is a reflection of her true self so it can be found consistently, though achieving this can be rather challenging.

A "yellow light" indicates to an athlete that she is a little off. This problem can be dealt with on the fly since she is not far from her "green light." Often, dropping an anchor like saying a key phrase to herself, looking at a particular reminder, or releasing the past by forgiving to forget will make the light "green." "Yellow light" indicators include traces of distraction, frustration, poor self-talk, or an inappropriate focus. Also, the re-emergence of a mechanical problem that was supposedly fixed in practice indicates a "yellow light." Basically, "yellow light" indicators are mild forms of "red light" indicators.

If an athlete wants to control her performance, she must first control herself. A "red light" indicates that she is significantly off from her ideal approach for performance. Therefore, she needs to stop what she is doing until the light becomes "green." The biggest difference between the traffic lights seen when driving a car and the traffic light checked on by athletes before performing is that the former changes to green on its own. In performance, it is the athlete's responsibility to actively make the light "green."

"Red light" indicators are specific to each athlete. Common signals include attitudes of frustration, anger, or impatience. Poor breathing patterns such as quick, shallow breathing may exist. Even failing to breathe is not uncommon. Other signals include time seeming to move faster than normal, excessive muscle tension, sweaty palms, a racing heart, dancing butterflies or an upset stomach, and many specific patterns of poor self-talk.

The following examples are common "green light," "yellow light," and "red light" indicators for softball players.

"Green Light" Indicators

- I'm confident.
- I feel strong and I'm relaxed.
- I'm having fun.
- Sternum up, chest out, shoulders back.
- Standing tall.
- "I've been here before and done well."
- I trust my plan of attack.
- I'm getting good results lately.

- I feel like the practice I've done is paying off.
- I feel the rhythm.
- I'm not thinking about much of anything.
- I'm seeing the game clearly and know what I want to do.
- I can sense what is going to happen just before it happens.
- I'm patient.
- Playing with an edge.
- Letting the game come to me.
- "I got this."
- Smooth
- Time seems slowed
- Feel unstoppable.

"Yellow Light" Indicators

- I'm thinking too much: c'mon, you can do this.
- I'm noticing too much: that fan sure is excited.
- I'm concerned: we really need this play.
- I'm frustrated: that was a ridiculous call.
- I'm frustrated: what's wrong with me?
- I should have gone the other way on that play.
- I'm making that mechanical mistake that I thought I had fixed again.

"Red Light" Indicators

- I'm thinking too much.
- I'm nervous—my heart is racing.
- My breathing is quick and shallow.
- I'm worried: "we need a win."
- I'm worried: "I'll lose playing time if I don't do well."
- I'm thinking about what will happen if we lose.
- I'm distracted by the past: that's not fair.
- I'm distracted by the past: I should've had that one.
- I'm thinking about hitting a home run.
- I screwed that play up because I rushed and my footwork got messed up.
- "She throws very hard."
- Not sure about what I want to try to do.
- I'm upset with myself.
- I'm upset by the situation.
- I'm frustrated.
- I'm impatient.
- I'm anxious.

- I'm bored.
- There are fielders everywhere. How am I going to find green space?
- I didn't see that play well.
- The game is going too fast.
- "I can't…"
- I'm not good enough.

EXERCISE

Make a list of your "red light," "yellow light," and "green light" indicators. You might start by circling the examples above that resonate for you. Record your list in Appendix B and then add to it or adjust it as awareness increases. Make separate lists for each performance situation.

<u>Warning:</u> Good and bad results and outcomes are the easiest indicators to list. They are appropriate, but since the goal is to eradicate a problem before it happens, make sure to also include indicators that will be available before the performance occurs, too.

All Lights Green (Gathering)

To flush the past completely out of consciousness, forget about it by focusing on what's next. If that doesn't work: FORGIVE to FORGET!

Gathering is the active process of turning personal "yellow light" or "red light" signals into "green light" "Go!" signals. It is the athlete's process of regaining control by taking charge of herself and her circumstance. To successfully gather, awareness is required. First, the athlete must know her personal "green light," "yellow light" and "red light" indicators. Then, she must check in with herself to see if all lights are green. If she notices a "yellow" or "red" signal, she actively uses a gathering strategy to make it "green" again. The distance she is from a "green light" will provide a good prediction about how much time it will take to successfully gather, though it is possible to change state in an instant. Fast change is achieved by dropping an anchor or by changing body language and thoughts (thereby changing physiology and attitude). Once self-control with a proper attitude and focus is reestablished, she is ready to perform.

Table 2-1

Red Light Indicators	Potential Gathering Strategy
I'm nervous and my heart is racing.	Slow down. I'm prepared. Use an affirming image, then do what I do.
My breathing is quick and shallow.	Take deep breaths.
I'm worried. We need this win.	A win would be good. Do my job!
I'm upset with myself.	Relax. Nobody's perfect.
I'm horrible.	I am good enough and things could start to fall my way on this next pitch.
The ball looks like a fast-moving pea.	Get locked in on the release point. Visualize it. See it big.
I'm thinking about what will happen if we lose.	Keep it here. One thing at a time.

Yellow Light Indicators	Potential Gathering Strategy
I'm thinking too much: "c'mon do this!"	Easy. Don't think. Just see it and do what I do.
I'm noticing too much: that fan sure is excited.	Tunnel vision: see it big.
I'm concerned: we really need a hit here.	A hit would be nice. What an opportunity!
Argh! I should have swung at that.	Be aggressive and trust the plan. It just takes one.
I'm striding slightly towards third base again.	Image (or practice) striding towards the pitcher. Check hype level and dial it down if necessary.

Awareness is the first step of gathering, because with awareness a change is possible. Next, each athlete must tailor her gathering strategy to meet her needs. Infinite differences exist, but one common strategy is a deep breath or two. During exhalation, the athlete should release unwanted tension in both her mind and her muscles. She must give her best effort to get to that trusting, thoughtless state that represents her "green light." Table 2-1 provides gathering possibilities for some "yellow light" and "red light" indicators listed previously. Each strategy can be sandwiched by a deep breath at the start and a reminder of what to focus on next at the end.

As athletes gain experience with their own traffic light signals, they will discover patterns. Certain situations will lead to specific variations in attitude or physiology, which will then be reflected in patterns of outcomes. Gaining this awareness is a key for consistency. With alertness and time, athletes know what to look for. Then, they develop strategies for making effective adjustments. Some of these steps will become part of their consistent pre-performance routine while others will be used only when a specific type of event throws her off track and creates the need.

Figure 2-3

Many athletes share similar "red light," "yellow light," and "green light" indicators, but every athlete's entire list of traffic light indicators will be unique for her in each performance situation. She should try to fill in each color with as many specific indicators as possible and then revise these lists often as her awareness increases. Memories dim with time, so some form of journaling is an important ingredient for maximizing awareness. If, in talking to someone or reading something (like this book), the athlete thinks, "That's me!" she should write it down. She does not want to lose that increase in clarity. The more detailed her "red light," "yellow light," and "green light" indicators, the better her awareness, adjustments, and performances will be. Awareness is the foundation skill upon which the entire mental side of the game is built.[3]

---

[3] See two superb awareness exercises: Appendix C – The Eight Mental Skills of Great Athletes Awareness Exercise and Appendix D – Leadership Assessment with 360° Feedback

CHAPTER 3

SMART WORK ROUTS HARD WORK 14-0 (DISCIPLINE)

Discipline yourself and others won't need to.
—John Wooden

Earn the right to be proud and confident.
—John Wooden

The harder you work, the harder it is to surrender.
—Vince Lombardi, Football Coach

Football is like life - it requires perseverance, self-denial, hard work, sacrifice, dedication and respect for authority.
—Vince Lombardi, Football Coach

Practice without improvement is meaningless.
—Chuck Knox, Football Coach

Excellence is not a singular act, but a habit. You are what you repeatedly do.
—Aristotle, Philosopher

Without self-discipline, success is impossible. Period.
—Lou Holtz, Football Coach

The road to Easy Street goes through the sewer.
—John Madden, Football Coach

You can never turn a switch on and off. It's got to always be on.
—Tiger Woods, Golfer

I'm a great believer in luck, and I find the harder I work the more I have of it.
—Thomas Jefferson, President, Author, and Educator

I believe in discipline. You can forgive incompetence. You can forgive lack of ability. But one thing you cannot ever forgive is lack of discipline.
—Forrest Gregg, Football Hall of Famer

> I found this sandbank by the Pearl River near my hometown, Columbia, Mississippi. I laid out a course on 65 yards or so. 65 yards on sand is like 120 on turf. But running on sand helps you make your cuts at full speed. I tried to pick the heat of the day to run in, but sometimes that sand will get so hot you can't stand in one place. It'll blister your feet. You get to the point where you have to keep pushing yourself. You stop, throw up, and push yourself again. There's no one around to feel sorry for you.
> —Walter Payton, Football Hall of Famer

To work smarter and improve faster, discipline is required. Discipline is commonly cited as a necessity for success in sports (or life). But what is discipline? How does an athlete know if she has a disciplined approach? Is it the sweat? The fatigue? The outcomes? Many young people (in age or maturity) lack a full and clear understanding of what it means to be disciplined. Laziness certainly shows a lack of discipline. Every great leader knows that she must go through the middle to get to the end. Quality practice is a necessity; it is the huge "middle." She cannot expect to coast through drills in practice and be able to "turn it on" in the game (or worse: late in the game if the score is close).

A leader works to make the performance in practice feel the same as it does in a playoff championship game. She goes game speed, or she does not go at all. Ideally, she cares equally about all of her results, regardless of the situation, because results always provide feedback about how well she is currently doing at approaching her potential (the "end" that she is striving for). She wants to be the best she can be and she knows that the only time she has any control over for reaching that lofty goal is right now. She has the discipline to move beyond her comfort zone, beyond her familiar zone. It is her habit of doing her best, now -- regardless of how hard that is -- that makes her successful.

Disciplined athletes make excellence second nature because they are willing to endure fatigue and pain now to enhance their pleasure later. Typically, this is pleasure that will result from performing better, maximizing her chances to win. Simply put, disciplined athletes are competitive. They run through the line instead of coasting to it. They go to bed at a decent hour rather than go out to a party. They lift weights rather than hang out in the weight room. They eat fruits and vegetables rather than fast food and ice cream. Their attitude is one of appreciation rather than one of entitlement. In many different ways, they push towards their goals rather than coasting along. Disciplined athletes figure out what their job is and do it the best they can.

Can a person work hard and still be undisciplined? Yes, and this is not uncommon. An athlete is mentally lazy if she does not constantly evaluate information, looking for the best way. Some athletes do not like to focus on the details. It is too much trouble, and after all, everyone can see that they are already working hard–just look at the sweat. Unfortunately, if they are working hard, but not smart, the return on their work will be less than a tenth of what it could be.

Quality practice produces improvement more than ten times faster than merely going through the motions. Slow progress occurs when the athlete does not work at the edge of her ability level, or she is not focused, or she works only on her strengths, not her weaknesses. Disciplined athletes understand the point of their practice, they focus their attention appropriately, and they wisely choose how to spend their time. Often, they spend most of their time working on their weaknesses and finish with their strengths (to maximize confidence and fun memories after practice). In the weight room, an athlete should train her proportionally weaker muscles more than her proportionally stronger muscles. Also, she should train for functional strength in her sport, not to look good on the beach. She takes the time to design drills that are as difficult or more difficult than the game situations that they simulate.

The same concept applies off the diamond. People are incredibly productive – sometimes. A big assignment might get procrastinated or, typically with the deadline looming, it might get completed in one evening. A musician can play through a new piece of music 100 times, repeating her mistakes. Then she gets inspired and practices just the most difficult tiny sections of the piece for a few hours and the effect is beautiful. A boss complains about her problems until she finally decides she "can't take it anymore." Then, she fixes them in a spurt of inspiration and perspiration. Are people doing better than their best? Emphatically, no! They are simply utilizing the power of discipline to race ahead. Smart work dominates the game of life, and if the score is kept, it would be a 14-0 blowout!

It is common for an athlete to practice the fun things first, neglecting the ones that seem harder. It is a good policy to attack the difficult things first and get them over with, then finish with the things that seem more enjoyable. Eventually, good habits will make difficult things seem less difficult, and it will be easier to enjoy the entire process. Therefore, "hard work" is a misnomer. Certainly the muscles will still feel pain and there will be struggles to reach new heights, but good habits breed more good habits. Challenges, obstacles, and pain can actually stop being perceived as difficult. Rather, they can become normal, productive requirements for success. What is difficult for the average athlete is routine for a champion.

Normal athletes' evaluations of what they are good at and what needs the most improvements are often biased by their expectations and prejudices. Most would rather protect their ego than identify a better way. When something goes wrong, they do not sufficiently search for the cause of the problem. When it is time to try something new, they hesitate or skip it because they fear the unknown. They do not know how to stretch their own boundaries. They have not learned to be comfortable being uncomfortable. As a result, they make poor adjustments and their rate of learning suffers, as does their performance in "uncomfortable" situations. Skillful adjustments and continuous learning are primary ingredients for any athlete/scientist to approach her potential.

Figure 3-1

The quality of an athlete's approach can be disciplined and unselfish or undisciplined and dictated by emotions and the selfish ego. A hitter should often go for a single to the opposite field rather than trying to pull a home run. The pitcher should execute a game plan rather than engage in a personal battle with the opposing 3-hole hitter. A lack of self-control causes athletes to act emotionally instead of rationally, which is often manifested in increased tension and/or aggressiveness. Examples of a lack of self-control include obvious mistakes such swinging at pitches that are not close to strikes or less obvious mistakes such as bad rhythm (usually rushing, but sometimes being too slow and careful) or loss of flexibility. Infinite examples exist. Discipline requires emotional control, thereby allowing the athlete to use her best judgment about how to maximize her chances of getting the outcomes she wants.

In the book *The Road Less Traveled: A New Psychology of Love, Traditional Values and Spiritual Growth*, Dr. M. Scott Peck clarified what it takes to have great discipline. His premise is that life is difficult, but with discipline, a person can transcend this difficulty. He breaks down discipline into four necessary components: delaying gratification, accepting responsibility, dedicating oneself to reality, and balancing. Delaying gratification means scheduling pain in the present to enhance pleasure in the future. Accepting responsibility involves recognizing that a problem any person is having is her problem and it is her job to solve this problem. Do not wait for someone else or "society" to fix it. Part of accepting responsibility involves a dedication to reality, which assumes a commitment to discovering truth or what is real and what is not. Stringent self-examination, willingness to be challenged, and relentless honesty are necessary components of a total dedication to reality. Shortcuts are sought for efficiency, but inappropriate shortcutting such as cheating is unacceptable. Finally, balancing, or choosing one course of action over another, requires flexibility, good judgment, and courage. It also acknowledges the pain of giving something up. In conclusion, Dr. Peck's work teaches that the disciplined individual is a spiritually evolved person who has the capability to transcend the difficulty of life.

Figure 3-2

All this information may seem like a lot for an athlete to handle. Do the details of good discipline make the attempt at it overwhelming? No. Would an effort to be disciplined be futile? Never. Clarification makes the process manageable, and the effort alone defines the success. All that is required is courage and motivation. Of course this is easier to understand than to do, but if courage and motivation exist, a leader will constantly fight to improve her skills. She will fall down often, but will get up each time. She will strive for perfection, but she will be smarter than to ever allow herself to expect it. She will keep the mountaintop in mind, sometimes at the forefront and often in the background, but she will enjoy the journey even more than the destination. By doing these things through motivated and courageous behavior, she will truly be disciplined in her attempt to approach her potential. Success is inevitable.

CHAPTER 4

YOUR GAME, YOUR ZONE (PEAK PERFORMANCE)

It was the best feeling ever. It was like I could do no wrong.

Maybe you can't play over your head at all.
Maybe it's just potential you never knew you had.
—Fran Tarkenton, Football Hall of Famer

Peak performances are awesome experiences. They should be sought, though not chased nor expected. When an athlete improves her mental skills, she increases her chance of having a peak performance and her chances at staying in the zone longer. Possessing mental toughness also means she is able to perform well when she is not at her best. Sport psychologist Ken Ravizza sums this last point up nicely when he challenges athletes to "learn to have a good, sh--ty day." The mental skills leaders use to get in the zone more often and perform better when they are not there are, fortunately, the same.

Awareness of what defines a peak performance is useful. Two descriptions of what many people would call an indescribable experience follow:

> *At the peak of tremendous and victorious effort, while the blood is pounding in your head, all suddenly becomes quiet within you. Everything seems clearer and whiter than before, as if great spotlights had been turned on. At that moment you have the conviction that you contain all the power in the world, that you are capable of everything, that you have wings. There is no more precious moment in life than this, the white moment, and you will work very hard for years just to taste it again.*
> —Yuri Vlasov, world champion weight lifter

> *When you're in the zone, you have switched from a training mode to a trusting mode. You're not fighting yourself. You're not afraid*

> *of anything. You're living in the moment in a special place and time. Athletes in the zone see everything with clarity. They are relaxed, they perform with a quiet mind with no indecision and no doubts. They can almost anticipate what is going to happen. They are totally absorbed.*
> —Gary Mack, sport psychologist and author

This book defines a peak performance as an extremely positive experience characterized by the mind and body working in harmony to achieve a process goal. In this experience, the athlete is totally engrossed in the moment; other considerations that could weigh on her mind temporarily cease to exist. There is no fear of failure. The athlete is energized but not anxious, narrowly focused on appropriate cues, and confident. She often feels like time has slowed down.

Confident, Not Cocky

Talent is God-given; be humble. Fame is man-given; be thankful. Conceit is self-given; be careful.

You expect success. You respect failure.
—Greg Norman, Golfer

When you're on top of your game, you don't take anything for granted.
—Sammy Sosa, Baseball Player

Once an athlete finds herself having a peak performance, she will want to stay there as long as possible. Unfortunately, inherent pitfalls are waiting for her at every turn, trying to bring her back "down to earth." While she is in the zone, she is, by definition, extremely confident. This confidence is super, but it is easy for her to become overconfident. When she is confident, she is tempted to think that she can do no wrong. She seems invincible, but if she is smart, she knows she is not. When she goes over the edge and becomes overconfident, she actually believes that the game is easy or that she is in some way invincible. Reality will bite her in the backside for this mistake, usually sooner rather than later.

The overconfident softball player makes assumptions and loses her edge. A hitter swings at everything, a fielder forgets to watch the ball into her glove, or a pitcher assumes that this pitch with two outs, nobody on, and the nine-hole hitter up is less important than other pitches. It is appropriate for the pitcher to have confidence that she can have a 1-2-3 inning, for the fielder to expect to catch the ball, or for the hitter to expect to hit it hard, but there is a limit. Knowing where that delicate balance lies is a tightrope act. With humility and alertness, awareness of how to avoid a bad fall can be acquired. This is all part of her learning process for approaching potential.

While searching for the balance of appropriate aggressiveness, an athlete can help maintain a peak performance by excusing mistakes as part of the normal process of learning her boundaries. The hitter's poor swing decision (e.g. swinging at a ball or a pitcher's pitch with less than two strikes) was bound to happen at some point, so she should not let that mistake bother her. She should certainly learn and adjust, but if she is bothered, she is likely to lose that zoned-in feeling. The emphasis of the mistake in her self-talk creates a feeling of concern, which is the opposite of the feeling she has when she is in the zone. Instead, she should maintain the fantastic, confident attitude that brought her to this point by focusing on what she learned and all the things she is doing correctly. Ultimately, she wants to maximize confidence – more is always better – without becoming cocky. She achieves this by respecting the difficulty of the game of softball (see Chapter 7).

> **The key for keeping super high confidence from ever becoming cockiness is respect for the game. It is never easy to give a best effort performance.**

To Care But Not Too Much

How many times have you started the season or, after a long layoff from the game, resumed golfing by shooting a score that was better than expected?
—Sam Snead, golfer

Olympian Scott Hamilton said he learned to approach his "most important" performances with "refined indifference." This was his method of freeing himself from any worry about outcomes. With the hard work of preparation successfully completed, a leader will enjoy those moments of high competition while having an intention, too. She knows what she wants to do, and she knows she is controlling everything she can, thus maximizing her chances for positive outcomes. She does not need to wait for these outcomes to occur to feel like a success because she defines success as Coach Wooden did. She is successful because of her process, not because of the outcomes that her behaviors lead to. She is detached, intentionally, from worries about the outcome. This perspective is often a challenging "green light" balance to maintain.

Developing refined indifference or intentional detachment, like all mental skills, can be practiced. The leader gets herself away from expectations. She avoids the words "should" and "supposed to." She might say, "I don't care…" over and over, adding phrases to make complete sentences such as: "I don't care what my Dad thinks" or "I don't care about things outside of my control." She might even get to the rare level of maturity that allows her true freedom from worry: "I don't care what happens on the scoreboard as long as I earn the peace of mind that comes from giving my best effort."

Creativity may be required to invent drills that allow athletes to practice this attitude. The following is an example of one such throwing drill that is quite simple: each pitcher is required to hit a target five times and is immediately penalized for missing (e.g. jog a lap around the field for the pitcher or her teammate). Pressure to hit the target increases as the athlete's desire to avoid the penalty grows; therefore, she must learn to stop being concerned with the penalty. The target should be hit by the pitchers when they are at their best between half and two-thirds of the time. In this drill, they will likely miss it more than normal. Some will miss it much more. The consequence of a miss is immediate. Whatever rules are set, no exceptions are allowed, and quitting is not an option.

This drill occasionally takes a long time. On one occasion, the collegiate athlete[4] had the reputation of having exceptional command (and great cardiovascular endurance – the penalty for each miss was approximately a 150 yard jog). He had a score of zero after his teammates had completed the assignment of hitting the target five times. Eventually, he yelled out in frustration, "Screw it, I don't care anymore!" Indeed, he hit the target on his very next attempt.

Leading by example[5] can be summarized by trying hard and executing three steps that lead to performing as well as possible: create an ideal internal state (attitude and physiology), commit to a plan of attack, and focus. An athlete's ideal state to approach her performance with is whatever works best for that individual. Typically, it includes confident, enthusiastic, aggressive, and relaxed. The plan of

---

[4] Sam Janda. The author was his coach.
[5] Leading by example and giving a best effort performance, even at practice, are synonymous. Go to http://www.coachtraub.com/images/pdfs/BestEffortPoster.pdf for a diagram summarizing what it takes to give a best effort performance, assuming that high motivation already exists, or use your QR Code Reader.

attack[6] is specific to the situation, aggressive under control, and positively worded. She commits to it by completely wanting to do what she is about to do. The focus is present-tense: engrossed in the task at hand. Many details of "strong mental skills" are presented in this book. Ultimately, they all boil down to these four steps: motivation, creating an ideal state, committing to the plan, and focusing with tunnel vision on the task at hand.

---

[6] Situation-specific softball strategy is outside of this book's scope. The importance of committing to a specific, controllable plan is not.

PART 2:

ATTITUDE, MEET ALTITUDE

Attitude determines altitude. Softball players agree that they play better when they are confident, aggressive, and enthusiastic and worse when they are frustrated, impatient, and not confident.

Attitude is a choice.

Attitudes are contagious. Make yours worth catching.

Morale and attitude are the fundamentals to success.
—Bud Wilkinson, Football Coach

Man does not simply exist, but always decides what her existence will be.... Every human being has the freedom to change at any instant. The last of the human freedoms is to choose one's attitude in any given set of circumstances, to choose one's own way.
—Viktor Frankl, in *Man's Search for Meaning*

Attitude has a huge, often underestimated, effect on every aspect of learning and performance. When pressed to address it, athletes know that they play significantly better with certain attitudes and significantly worse with others. The dictionary defines attitude as someone's "manner, feeling, disposition, position, etc. with regard to a person or thing; tendency or orientation, especially of the mind." An athlete's attitude reflects her emotional state and is correlated to her physiological state, so to control her attitude, she must control her emotions and her body as well. Athletes can, though it is not easy, create an ideal performance state in any situation by learning to control their attitude and their physiology.

Most people do not control their attitude most of the time. Leaders control their attitude almost always. They understand the relationship between their self-talk (their perspective on life, the way they explain their experiences and environment to themselves) and their attitude. Then, they choose to emphasize the thoughts that are most useful for helping them get what they want. These thoughts are often not the most logical, likely, or convenient, but they are both true and useful.

Leaders then take it one more step. They know that when their teammates have a good attitude, they become more optimistic, coachable, persistent, and effective, so they find a way to fill up their emotional tanks. They do this first by having contagious positive energy. Next, they make others feel valued. They also help their teammates emphasize true thoughts that are useful and de-emphasize damaging thoughts, whether they are true or false. They support through the tough times and push carefully in situations when that is needed, such as conditioning, weight training, or long practices. Often, they push without words by their example. Sometimes they speak up, not with the fear of offending or being out of order, but with careful attention to whether their words are effective or not. Leaders put the needs of the team ahead of their personal desires or fears, and they know that helping their teammates have fun and stay confident is a priority on their team's list of needs.

Chapter 5

She Wants It So Bad

The difference between a successful person and others is not a lack of strength,
not a lack of knowledge, but rather a lack of will.
—Vince Lombardi, Football Coach

To win you must have desire and talent—but desire is first.
—Sam Snead, Golfer

The only thing that counts is your dedication to the game.
You run on your own fuel; it comes from within you.
—Paul Brown, Football Coach

The will to win, the desire to succeed, the urge to reach your full potential... these are the
keys that will unlock the door to personal excellence.
—Confucius, Philosopher

Coach Ronny Feldman is a superlative football coach at Blinn College in Texas, one of the top junior college programs in the country. He tells this story:

We got this highly touted quarterback here in January. On the first day of workouts, we really try to work the guys hard. We're all over them in the weight room and conditioning and when we're done, they're exhausted. We want to show them how tough it's going to be to reach our goal of a National Championship next fall. Afterwards, this quarterback comes over to me and asks for a bag of balls. He says he and a couple of guys want to play catch and sure enough, he has talked two guys into staying after for some extra work.

The next day it's the same thing, only this time he's got a half dozen guys with him. On the third day, he also asks for the playbook and he has over a dozen guys out there learning the plays! It was like this every day. This guy was totally respectful and humble. He always wanted to learn more and his motor just never stopped. As I

> watched him lead us in the off-season, I was thankful because I knew Cam Newton was taking us to the 2009 Championship.[7]

Motivation is a big deal. Leaders like Cam Newton have amazing levels of energy. This is not because they are better at metabolizing sugars or genetically predisposed for hard work, it is because they are more motivated to tap into the deep reserves of energy that are part of the human condition. The key to unlock the door to these reserves is attitude.

Leaders are competitive. Wanting to do well can have negative effects like pressing, tension, and a less-than-best-effort performance, but when it is time to go to work, an athlete cannot be too competitive. No athlete works her hardest all the time, and no athlete will approach her potential without a great deal of disciplined work. Approaching potential for an athlete means doing her best, which takes as much smart work as possible. This is a lofty goal. Great coaches inspire their athletes to action. The most important coach any athlete has is herself. Therefore, to approach their potential, leaders find a way to inspire and motivate themselves first. This allows them to set the example necessary to inspire others. Like bathing, a daily dose of motivation is recommended.

How does a leader motivate herself? First, by recognizing the truth about how powerful she is. Things can go well for her and they can go poorly, but if she learns to consistently tap into her personal power by "winning" the mental side of the game, they will go well much more often.

Motivated is an attitude and attitudes come from thoughts, so she gets herself motivated by focusing on particular thoughts. Perhaps she imagines how great it will feel to give her best effort when the lights are brightest. Does she have a chip on her shoulder? Many athletes are motivated by their need to prove themselves. Does she fear letting herself or others down? Maybe remembering the alternative way of spending her time will convince her to make the most of this opportunity. Does her competitiveness drive her? If so, she can simply remind himself of the importance of what she is going to do. Or is it the potential rewards? She might think about the effects of doing her best. Perhaps avoiding negative consequences keeps her going. There are specific keys for every athlete and with awareness, a daily strategy for staying motivated can be built.

Coach Wooden told athletes to discipline themselves so that others would not need to. Some athletes love to perform because they want to impress others? Think of

---

[7] Blinn College football won the 2009 junior college national championship. Newton also won a national championship at Florida in 2008 as a backup and another at Auburn in 2010.

who might be watching today, or simply imagine that someone important is watching. Leaders know that they do not want to do anything different when that important person shows up. Some athletes truly hate to lose. This is common in many world-class athletes, so they find a way to train better than their competition today. They simply will not be denied. Those who are the most skilled at motivating themselves will possibly fool others into thinking that their motivation is simply built into their genetic code, but it is their ability to focus their thoughts on their personal "go" button(s) that creates that internal drive. Certainly this comes easier for some and harder for others, but "go, go, go" is an attitude available to everybody.

Figure 5-1

Alertness provides awareness of what motivates. Some athletes prefer to go with the flow rather than stay alert, because paying attention to all the details of life requires discipline. It can seem to be too tiring. With alertness, an athlete will notice patterns about the times when she was extremely productive and those times when she was lazy. She will notice conditions surrounding specific events in which she pushed forward consistently, and she will learn about times when she coasted. Perhaps she tried to "turn it on" after coasting through the first half of a game, could not do so, and became so upset that she announced, "That will never happen again!" If this proclamation worked, great. If she did not follow up on it, she learned that an adjustment is needed. It is never appropriate for her to beat herself up over being less than perfect, yet that is no reason not to strive for perfection. She should pay attention, recognize where she is and where she wants to be, and give her best effort to get there. Awareness is the foundation for effective adjustments.

The Energizer Bunny

To be the very best you can be, you have to have the intellect. My body just does what my mind tells it to. Losers quit. When you have a sound mind, you can do what is necessary.
—Evander Holyfield, Boxer

I'll never look back and say that I could have done more. I've paid the price in practice, and I know I get the most out of my ability.
—Carl Yastrzemski, Baseball Hall of Famer

Describing a competitor as *relentless* is very high praise. To be consistently pushing forward, a leader must first know her own motivational strengths and weaknesses. Everyone has weaknesses, but not everyone allows what comes naturally to dictate her behavior. If something does not work, leaders change it. Does she sometimes play down to the level of her competition? Does she tend to become a bit lazy during "less important" games? Does she coast because she believes that she will be able to "turn it up a notch" late in the game? Is her play uninspired when her team is way ahead or way behind? If she coasts for any reason, then her primary goal is not to simply "do her best." Adjust! The relentless competitor's motto is, "best effort – one play at a time." Does she appreciate the importance of practice? Does she take care of her body with good nutrition, weight training, flexibility work, stress management, and time management? With awareness, an athlete can make appropriate adjustments and close the gap between potential and performance.

Figure 5-2

Games are exciting. In addition to the thrill of competition with others, each game provides wonderful feedback about how well the athlete is competing with herself. She has to be able to discern relevant from irrelevant information, but both uncontrollable outcomes and controllable results teach her about the quality of her approach in practice and in the game.

A leader who is having trouble getting relentlessness up to the level she wants will seek assistance. Then, she will repeat what works and change or drop strategies that do not. Perhaps a competitor, friend, supervisor, colleague, coach, or family member motivates her. If so, she will go out of her way to spend time with that person. Or perhaps her key is a book, a song, or a saying. Maybe a new habit of reading or reciting the right words at the right times would keep her motivated. Taking the time at the beginning (of the day, practice, etc.) to set her intentions with a few minutes of meditative imagery is extremely powerful. Ultimately, she must know her job and do her job the best she can right now. Do it once, do it again, and do it again, and notice that it gets easier as momentum is established.

Persistence will get an athlete to her goal. A lack of it will keep her from it. "Relentlessness is a good quality. I don't care what you do for a living," said baseball manager Tony LaRussa. Pushing forward all the time is too much to ask of most people, but athletes who can do it get rewarded. The Energizer Bunny-type at practice is the coach's pet for a reason: she gets more done! When most athletes' body language and attitude say, "I'm tired," hers says, "What else?"

Can she persevere through adversity? Does she have the inner confidence to say, "Keep going. I will get it done!" Does she have the will to win? There's a big difference between saying she wants these things and acting that out, although saying it is certainly the first step. Industrialist and philanthropist Andrew Carnegie said, "The average person puts only 25% of his energy and ability into his work. The world tips its hat to those who devote more than 50% of their capacity, and stands on its head for those few and far between souls who devote 100%."

EXERCISE

Self-assess your relentlessness at the end of each practice by giving yourself a relentlessness grade on a scale of 1-100 for today. Then, at the beginning of the next day, remember the grade you gave yourself yesterday and set a goal that is a bit higher. Of course the ideal is to strive for perfection – 100%, but if that is not realistic (since humans have flaws), do not expect it. One appropriate strategy is to make a goal for today that is 5% higher than yesterday's score.

Going Somewhere?

> You never achieve real success unless you like what you are doing.
> —Dale Carnegie, Author and Teacher

> Success is a journey not a destination. The doing is usually more important than the outcome. Not everyone can be number 1.
> —Arthur Ashe, Tennis Player

> Everybody is looking for instant success, but it doesn't work that way. You build a successful life one day at a time.
> —Lou Holtz, Football Coach

A mission is the athlete's overall goal for her sporting experience, her purpose for playing. What drives her? It is a good idea for much of the mission to be controllable and one goal that is always controllable is to discover her potential by consistently doing her best. It is a lofty goal, but the journey of a thousand miles begins with a single step. Leaders have a destination in mind, but do not need the entire path illuminated. They merely need to be able to see the next step.

Keeping her mission in mind, sometimes on the surface of consciousness and sometimes at a deeper level, promotes relentlessness. Many people avoid clarity because they fear "failure." If these people defined success and "failure" appropriately, then this fear would dissipate. Both success and "failure" lie in the effort, not in the outcome. Success is "the peace of mind that comes from knowing you did your best," while real failure occurs only when the competitor fails to try. The wisdom in these statements becomes apparent with the pursuit of the question of why these definitions are valid. As Mahatma Gandhi said, "Full effort is full victory."[8]

Leaders do not need a safety net. They know that their best is all they can do. Most athletes prefer the net. They do not give their best effort because if they do not achieve a goal, they can take solace in knowing that they could have tried harder. Those who define success with outcomes, give their best effort and fall short feel horrible. From their perspective, they are failures. It is simply safer to hold back.

Zoe Koplowitz, who has multiple sclerosis, is an example of a leader who kept her mission in mind. With the aid of two custom-made canes, Zoe completed her mission of walking the New York City Marathon. The marathon took her 28 hours, after which she had the following to say:

---

[8] Most athletes, especially under 25 years old, disagree: they think if the team lost, it cannot be a full victory.

Either you have your dreams, or you live your dreams. I'm not all that remarkable. I just keep putting one foot in front of the other until I get to where I have to go. Everybody's got their finish line in life. This is mine. People need to know that success isn't all about winning.

> ## EXERCISE
>
> Write down your mission. In one or two sentences, explain why you compete? Next, record how you would like to be remembered at your retirement party. What would you like your peers to say about you? Finally, record your definition of a successful season. If you achieve that success this year and similar ones in future years, it should logically follow that you will succeed in achieving your mission. (Answers to these long-term questions begin the process of setting optimally effective goals, which is the challenge of Chapter 22.)

CHAPTER 6

CHAMPIONS LOOK AT IT THIS WAY

It is much easier to see the picture when you are not inside the frame.

The grass isn't greener on the other side. It's greener where you water it.

There's no substitute for hard work. If you work hard and you prepare yourself as an athlete and you are in great shape, you might get beat, but you'll never lose.
—Nancy Lieberman-Cline, Basketball Player

Everything we see is a perspective, not the truth.
—Marcus Aurelius, Roman Emperor

Don't measure yourself by what you have accomplished, but by what you should have accomplished with your ability.
—John Wooden

I am a winner. I just didn't win today.
—Greg Norman, Golfer

If you make every game a life-and-death proposition, you're going to have problems. For one thing, you'll be dead a lot.
—Dean Smith, Basketball Coach

For any athlete to perform up to her potential, it is vital for her to focus effectively. It is difficult, for example, to hit a target that she does not see. Therefore, the way she focuses—her perspective—is critical. The dictionary defines perspective as the "ability to see things in a true relationship" to one another or a "specific point of view in understanding things or events." Another definition says "the appearance of objects as determined by their relative distance and positions." Synonyms are outlook, attitude, and aspect. Athletes find all sorts of ways to hold themselves back from performing at their best; most of these are related to a flawed perspective, or flawed patterns of self-talk.

Two separate ideas about perspective exist. First is the athlete's Weltanschauung, which is her overall world view. Her priorities. This angle on perspective is discussed in this chapter. The second is specifics of the view she has when she looks at something, or her focus, which is the topic of Part 4 of this book. Healthy priorities and views about life's events affect each other. To consistently perform near her best, an athlete must learn to look at life in a way that is both true and useful. True, because she will not be able to lie to herself. Useful, because there are two sides to every coin. Both sides are true, but only one is most useful. For example, it is more useful to view the glass as half full than half empty.

An attitude of gratitude is a key skill for success in softball, as in life. Being thankful improves the heart's rhythmic functioning, which reduces stress, promotes clarity of thought, and aids the healing process. It is physiologically impossible to feel stressful and grateful at the same time. Grateful athletes are more relaxed, more coachable, more forgiving, more present to the task at hand, and generally more positive than their counterparts. They are less likely to complain. Author Jon Gordon says, "Remember that complaining is like vomiting. Afterwards you feel better but everyone around you feels sick." Leaders live out the words of John Wooden, "Don't whine. Don't complain. Don't make excuses."

Athletes love to be "in rhythm" and this is much more likely to happen when they are "in gratitude." They might consider the belief that they "won the lottery" when they were born. Winning the lottery means gaining immense wealth at odds of roughly 10,000,000 to 1. Americans today have some real problems, without a doubt, but when compared to all the present and past times and places that people could have been born, they are extremely lucky to have been born when and where they were. The odds of being born with this many opportunities for health, freedom, happiness, contribution, and satisfaction are many, many times longer than the odds of winning the lottery!

Athletes who are trying to find their ideal performance state certainly should consider an attitude of gratitude as one of their significant "green" light indicators. Instead of focusing on the pressure and the consequences of mistakes, gratitude promotes a focus on playing the game the right way for the right reasons. Instead of pressure and disappointing people, leaders focus on opportunities, including the opportunity to make themselves proud.

An unhealthy perspective in softball says "win at all costs; the score is the only concern." The first step to a healthy perspective on the game is to recognize that it is just a game. Softball is not a life-or-death proposition. Parents and other loved ones will not stop loving because of what happens on the field today. Athletes in "big" moments on television may have literally millions of eyes on them and they are sometimes "tough" enough to perform as though they have not a care in the world. Attend a little league softball game and you are likely to see a few nine-year-olds carrying the weight of the world on their shoulders. The source of these polar opposites is not the situation, but the way the athlete perceives the situation. Her healthy perspective is what will empower her with the freedom to be totally engrossed in the moment, allowing her to perform her best under pressure and making her the kind of athlete that others want to follow.

Figure 6-1

This is not to say that a leader is not competitive. On the contrary, she is extremely competitive. Winning is always more fun than losing and if she is going to play the game, she is going to play to win, including at practice each day. It is a silly question to ask which team "wants it more" in the finals of a tournament. That question has already been clearly answered in the way the two teams prepared themselves at practice. Both teams "want it" badly when the prize is right in front of them. Leaders "want it" just as badly when the prize is off in the distance and their current job is painful.

Winning is far better than the alternative, but the "winning is absolutely critical" perspective is a problem because it does not encourage effort if the victory can be obtained easily. It also does not encourage effort if maximal effort is not perceived to be likely to lead to winning. In fact, it (often subconsciously) discourages it because the person who loses without maximal effort can still defend her win-driven ego (unhealthy perspective) by believing that if she had tried harder, she *might* have won. However, if she took the chance of giving maximal effort and did not get the desired outcome, she would have no solace. She would feel like a "failure." Not giving her best effort is, she believes, her safest course of action. ~~Many athletes~~… Most athletes need and keep this safety net for their psyche. Leaders do not know what will happen, but because of their perspective on success, they do not need a safety net. They know that their best effort is always good enough.

Mistakes are Good

Make learning most important today.

It's important to know that at the end of the day it's not the medals you remember. What you remember is the process—what you learn about yourself by challenging yourself, the experiences you share with other people, the honesty the training demands— those are things nobody can take away from you whether you finish twelfth or you're an Olympic champion.
—Silken Laumann, Olympic Bronze Medalist

A healthy perspective on sports reflects the definitions of success and "failure" promoted throughout this book. Success is "the peace of mind that comes from knowing you did your best." "Failure" is a term others use to describe undesirable outcomes, but those are not really bad. "Failure" is simply part of the process of achieving success. Real failure (without quotation marks) is bad and can only happen with the athlete's permission. It includes various forms of quitting and excuses.

Figure 6-2

This set of priorities encourages effort towards best-possible behaviors. It emphasizes the process of athletes practicing and performing and doing their best. It acknowledges the importance of destinations, but emphasizes enjoyment for the journeys to these destinations. The leader's journey is most important because personal growth and the welfare of the team are her primary concerns. Improvements come from effort. Full attention to the task at hand is valued because an ideal focus leads to growth. Most importantly for enhancing performance, freedom from anxiety about outcomes makes it possible for an athlete to consistently enjoy the process of performing during games. Through both tough times and smooth sailing, athletes with a healthy perspective will play with a freedom of spirit that allows them to perform up to their potential.

An ideal perspective recognizes that more important things in life exist than today's performance. This does not mean that performance outcomes do not matter. In addition to their effects on little things like status, money, and reputation (wink, wink), outcomes provide a competitor with feedback about her process. They are important because they reveal the truth about what works and what does not. However, no single outcome should ever be given too much importance. No loss should ever be seen as a catastrophe. No "failure" should be allowed to carry an emotional scar of inadequacy. No fear of "failure" will interfere with performance because a competitor with a healthy perspective on the game knows that by putting forth great effort, she cannot fail. She will be a success in her own eyes and the eyes of those who watch her with a healthy perspective. In fact, she already is successful if she designs, practices, and executes her plans (routines) to the best of her ability. The stress and pressure to perform that others feel is replaced only by the pressure she puts on herself to perform up to her potential as quickly as possible.

Figure 6-3

Every athlete will experience many challenges and setbacks along her journey to find out how good she can be. With a healthy perspective, she will view each obstacle as a stepping-stone to success. Challenges and pitfalls provide motivation for her to do better next time; they are not viewed as a disappointment or "failure." She is finding out which things work so she can repeat them and which things could be done better so she can change them. Most people view outcomes as bad or good, but leaders view them as bad and good. Yes, mistakes are good.

To promote growth, a strong-minded athlete is extremely coachable. She welcomes coaches' feedback and even seeks out constructive criticisms. Most athletes avoid or ignore criticisms because the identification of the mistake within the criticism makes them *feel* like a "failure." They do not like any negative feedback, even if it is constructive, appropriate, and polite. This response is emotional, not rational. All that is needed to adjust it is a decision to use the brain.

Figure 6-4

An athlete with a healthy perspective is a great teammate. She works hard and has a consistently positive attitude, plus she looks to help others. She admires those who excel, rather than criticizing them. In fact, she has a personal rule against ever criticizing a teammate in public. She has no interest in competing with her own teammates. Rather, she encourages and complements them. She is patient with those who struggle, knowing that she, too, has weaknesses. Everyone's strengths and weaknesses are different. She is encouraging and optimistic when times are tough and comfortable expressing her joy and appreciation when times are good. Her teammates enjoy her presence.

A leader's attitude towards a "clutch" moment in competition is another impressive part of her mental game. She views every performance as an opportunity to evaluate and display all the work she has done to prepare. Others may focus on the pressure, but she knows that increased pressure is the shadow of increased opportunity. This opportunity is her chance to "show off" to herself (especially), her family, and others the combination of her talents and her efforts.

The bigger stage is the better stage, as far as she is concerned, because she is proud of her preparation and her ability. In fact, she lives for that big moment that follows the thought, "Bring it on! I'm ready and I know I will succeed because I know I will give my best effort."

Figure 6-5

Who are you playing this weekend? The best answer is "ourselves." In a big game, a mentally tough athlete's confidence is doubled by her superb mental skills and that of her teammates. She is doubtful that her opponents have such a healthy perspective on the game or that they are as thoroughly prepared as she and her team, both physically and mentally. The ironic truth is that the person who wants to produce positive outcomes because she defines her success by her achievement is much less likely than the person with a healthy perspective to get that good outcome. So it is: trying to win by outscoring the other team decreases the chance of that happening; trying to win versus oneself increases the chance of scoring more than the other team. This is because at the performance level, the unhealthy competitor does not know how to focus effectively. She has too much to worry about, especially as the pressure rises. She does not know if she will be comfortable looking at herself in the mirror after the game. The healthy athlete knows.

No Achievement Necessary?!?

Thank you for teaching me that my best is good enough.
—Andre Agassi, Tennis Player

You must sacrifice, train, do everything possible to put yourself in a position to win. But if you consider second or third a failure, I feel sorry for you.
—Joe Falcon, Runner (mile in 3:49:31)

You cannot live a perfect day without doing something for someone who will never be able to repay you.
—John Wooden

So many people get their identity through sports, and we have to remember that's what they do, not who they are.
—Pat Summitt, Basketball Coach

It is very, very dangerous to have your self-worth riding on your results as an athlete.
—Jim Courier, Tennis Player

For when that One Great Scorer comes
To mark against your name,
He writes – not that you won or lost
But how you played the game.
—Grantland Rice, Football Coach

Why is a less-than-ideal perspective normal? Why is it so common that today's athletes hold the distorted belief that success depends on achievement? Why would athletes wrap their self-worth around their daily sport performances? Because unless they are careful, socialization into the American competitive, capitalist culture will teach them that the outcomes are what matters most.

Many people, organizations, and critics knowingly or unwittingly promote the idea that it is appropriate to "win at all costs." The media rewards achievement and makes "larger-than-life superstars" out of those athletes who put up superior numbers. "Just win, baby" says the advertisement or commentator. Rewards such as money and adulation are given out for positive outcomes in competition, without regard for the sources of those outcomes (steroids, academic shortcuts, illegal recruiting). Because they are similarly socialized, parents, peers, "role models," and coaches sometimes reinforce the terrible concept that athletes are good people when they produce good outcomes but are of little or no value when they do not.

Unless an athlete succeeds in ignoring this bad influence, socialization will create a performance/self-concept link in her mind that now needs to be broken. Children are captive to their environment. Adults are captive to their habits, but human adults are uniquely gifted with the ability to create new habits. The softball player who acts like an adult has somehow learned that her value as a person does not depend on winning a game. In fact, it does not depend on anything other than being born. It is an immeasurably immense birthright.

Figure 6-6

Self-esteem (discussed more in Chapter 8) is not a given; it is the reputation a person acquires of herself. Self-esteem is not based on achievements in softball. On the contrary, it depends on many factors, including the care an athlete demonstrates for family, herself, and others. Her work-ethic, including her ability to find the truth, accept responsibility, and take appropriate actions is critical. Self-esteem also depends on her integrity and the effort she puts forth to reach her goals. Her integrity is completely intact when her words, thoughts, and actions all line up with each other in accordance with her values[9]. Self-esteem can be thought of as global confidence; it is a direct factor in an athlete's confidence (and therefore performance) in any situation.

The "American way" highly regards achievement for good reasons. First, positive outcomes typically reflect a superior effort. Second, winning feels great, so people naturally want to win or be associated with those who do. Last, it is easier to measure an objective score than someone's subjective effort. Speed is objective; "intangibles" are subjective. Batting average and runs scored are clear; the team concept demonstrated by a leader is unclear.

---

[9] See Appendix E – Values Exercise

The importance of winning can be a great thing because it motivates. Winning, particularly against high-level competition, is enabled by a strong mental game. Therefore, those athletes who want to win badly enough will figure out what works and do it. Problems arise when shortcomings in perspective and self-esteem put up a roadblock to growth. All roadblocks can be passed, but this process can be painful and it requires awareness. This awareness might only be found with the assistance of a friend, parent, coach, or even a therapist or counselor. To avoid this pain, many roadblocks are not passed. Every athlete is a product of her genetics and her environment, but with discipline, she can assume adult responsibilities, keeping the positives and breaking the chains of any negative environmental effects. Clearly, it is not just experiences that matter, but what is done with these experiences.

If people all had equal genetic abilities and environmental support (including luck), the score would accurately reflect effort. This is not the world we live in. Every person has different abilities, different strengths, and different weaknesses. A person strong in some skills (physical or mental) will be weak in other areas. The person who can run the fastest may be weakest in maintaining a positive, confident attitude. In fact, that great "athlete" from high school may be the most disadvantaged one: her physical gifts are so easy to see that the expectations of others are set high. Meanwhile, her mental shortcomings tend not to be understood or coached very well. She will get away with many mental mistakes because of her physical talent until the level of competition becomes high enough to expose these shortcomings. She is bound for an emotional roller coaster that may have some serious rough spots. On the other hand, it is comical that some people call Peyton Manning, Whitney Canion, or Craig Counsell poor athletes. They not only have above-average physical skills but also have world-class mental skills.

Hopefully, the position each athlete loves takes advantage of her strengths and minimizes her weaknesses. This tends to happen more than chance might suggest because athletes pursue roles where they have "success." However, there are also many times when an environmental factor caused the athlete to pursue something that she was not "made" for. Some people want to be part of a team and do not like to be the center of attention or primarily responsible for how well things are going. This personality type is a problem for a pitcher, even if her loving father started teaching her to pitch at age five. Honesty about what is fun and what goals are realistic will lead the athlete to wonderful pursuits.

EXERCISES

Exposing the Core of Your Relationship with Softball

1. What percentage of the time is your best effort likely to be good enough? All answers are valid, but only one answer is best for consistent excellence in performance.

2. Why do you invest time, money, sweat, and tears into softball? Why do you compete? Record your answer, and then write down why you want that. Continue repeating why you want that, persistently forcing honesty until you get to the core components of softball that hold the greatest value for you.

3. Self-Acceptance comes from a refusal to be in an adversarial relationship with yourself. It is a foundational step of healing mental challenges and diseases. What are one or two things that you might be tempted to deny about your body, your core values, or your habits?

4. Tap into the knowledge you already possess by doing sentence completion exercises to build your self-esteem. Complete each sentence in as many grammatically correct ways as possible in five minutes. Do not worry about the logic or value of each sentence. Simply make each sentence you record grammatically correct.
   - Living consciously means to…
   - If I bring 5% more awareness to my softball activities today, I might notice that I…
   - If I bring 5% more awareness to my insecurities today, I might notice that I…
   - If I bring 5% more awareness to my priorities today, I might notice that I…
   - If I bring 5% more attention to how I deal with people today, I might notice that I…
   - If anything I have been saying is true, it might be a good idea if I…

CHAPTER 7

DO NOT RESPECT THE OPPONENT...
RESPECT THE GAME

There is a hell of a difference between doing it almost right and doing it right.
—Bobby Knight, Basketball Coach

When you lose a couple of times, it makes you realize how difficult it is to win.[10]
—Steffi Graf, Tennis Player

Anytime you give a man something he doesn't earn, you cheapen him.
Our kids earn what they get, and that includes respect.
—Woody Hayes, Football Coach

It is not necessary to respect the opponent to give a best effort performance. It is necessary to respect that giving a best effort performance is always challenging. It requires diligent preparation, creating an ideal state, committing to a quality plan, and an intense focus, one step at a time. Athletes who excel may not always respect their opponent, but they always respect their sport.

What does it mean to "respect the game?" The respectful athlete is committed to improving her skills, and she practices and plays with intensity. She is humble, recognizing that the game is difficult and acknowledging that it should be difficult. It is precisely this difficulty that makes a contest between two respectful teams a beautiful event to behold. Expecting challenges, the competitors exert maximum effort. They understand that the most important play in the game is this next one; therefore, their mantra is to "give my best effort, one play at a time." They have prepared and continue to work hard and smart to overcome adversity as they put their talents and perseverance on display.

---

[10] Well said, Steffi. This is a critical lesson and clear example of why losing is not just bad, it is also good!

Athletes demonstrate intensity in a variety of ways. The intense athlete tends to "little things" in a way that reflects an understanding that there are no "little things." Everything is a "big thing" because the slightest edge can make the difference on any one play and any one play can impact the outcome of the game. Even if it does not directly impact the score, each play is an opportunity to either keep the momentum or get it back. The intense athlete never takes the routine play for granted; she gets herself ready for every pitch. Sometimes this readiness includes a positive expectation that whatever can help will happen—even if it is statistically unlikely. Everything is an opportunity for something, and leaders always expect that something to be something good.

This positive outlook includes responses to adversity. If the other team makes a great play, a leaders trusts that it will take more than that to defeat her and her teammates. She is not bothered by an umpire's or a teammates' mistake; she knows how to focus on the next pitch. If the other team gets out to a quick 5-0 lead, the respectful athlete thinks that if they can score that fast, so can we. Then she acts in a way on this next play to try to provide a spark by doing her job to the best of her ability. Perhaps this play will provide the opportunity for her to grab the momentum for her team.

Figure 7-1

Intense players hustle relentlessly, playing the game both aggressively and under control. Fielders are ready to react quickly on each pitch, even if the ball is unlikely to be hit in their direction. Baserunners do not assume that they will be out or that they know what will happen next. They know what to anticipate (line drive, wild pitch/passed ball) and how to be patient and react to what they see. A great hitter who gets the sacrifice bunt sign is not just willing, but actually eager to get the bunt down. When she is allowed to swing away, she expects a good pitch to hit, but has defined what that is so she can succeed at taking other pitches. Outfielders move on every play, reacting to the ball, backing up throws, and being ready to help out in any way possible. Infielders are quick, but they do not hurry, which could cause a fumbled ball or errant throw. Leaders are ready so that if their opponent leaves the door open even a crack, they will walk on through. In summary, the player who respects the game has a disciplined approach to playing all out, one play at a time. For fans, it is a joy to watch respectful leaders perform.

Never Ass-u-me

> I never underestimate an opponent. A guy might be small in stature,
> but he can be very tough inside.
> —Carl Banks, Football Player

Great athletes do not play up or down to the situation, they play up to the game of softball. They assume nothing. They recognize the importance of giving their best effort every time. This philosophy eliminates many potential hazards to their attitude and performance. They do not give their opponent too much or too little credit. If the opponent has a great reputation, great competitors know that if they play their best, it is likely that the opponent will "flinch." Their confidence may get that athlete with the great reputation "off" of her game. In an unspoken way, leaders send the message that they will give nothing away today. If they lose, it will be because the opponent earned the victory. They also know that their opponent's performance is out of their control, so they do their best and accept whatever happens. All they can do is all they can do. And regardless of the opponent's performance today, the outcomes will certainly be more to their liking if they perform near their best.

On the other end of the spectrum, leaders will not take positive outcomes against an underdog opponent for granted, nor will they be satisfied with a big, early lead. They are confident but not cocky. Part of respecting the game includes respecting not the opponent per se, but at least respecting the possibility that if the opponent happens to have a good day today (or the rest of the day), victory will not come easily. More to the controllable point, they realize that doing their best can never come easily. If they assume an easy victory, their hype level will be too low. This lack of intensity certainly might open the door for a potential upset.

On the smaller scale of a single play, respectful athletes will never view any task as too easy (or "routine") to deserve their full attention and focus. When respect is absent, the word "routine" often leads to careless mistakes. Indeed, they are "careless"—not enough care was taken to make the play. Leaders make both ordinary and extraordinary plays appear easy. They execute not with cockiness but with confidence and respect. They know their job is to get themselves ready to perform physically and mentally, to commit to the plan of attack, and to focus and finish each play. Leaders do not skip steps in doing their job.

Figure 7-2

Sir James Matthew Barrie, the author of *Peter Pan*, calls life "a long lesson in humility." Softball is like life. When athletes perform well, they often become over-confident. If they are not open to criticism, someone else will learn faster. If they are not respectful of others, they forfeit chances at the teamwork it takes to approach potential. Even in individual sports, athletes are more powerful with the support of others.

Consistency is the goal. If athletes are not intense in their approach because they start believing the game is not too difficult, they cease to give their best effort each step of the journey. If they lose their sense of urgency because they deny the possibility that this opponent or game is capable of beating them today, they sometimes get lucky -- but often pay a hefty price. Why take that chance (and build poor habits in the process)?

Does the importance of humility defy the importance of confidence or interfere with aggressiveness? No! Leaders are confident, aggressive, and humble. They respect that both softball and giving a best effort performance are always difficult. Performing consistently requires balance. Leaders fall over less frequently than others because they maintain a hunger to learn and an eagerness to work. Their preparation is superior. Outcomes have ups and downs because people, by definition, are imperfect. However, with a disciplined, humble approach, leaders perform well even when they are not at their best and their peak performances occur more frequently and last longer. Their humility breeds their consistency!

Chapter 8

Am I Talking To Myself? Am I Good at It?

Change your thoughts and change your world.
--Norman Vincent Peale, Author of *The Power of Positive Thinking*

The greatest discovery of my generation is that human beings can alter their lives by altering their attitudes.
--William James, Psychologist

If you want to be a success in life you must believe in yourself and encourage yourself through your self-talk.
—Anonymous

Changing your self-image can change your life. Changing your self-image begins with changing your self-talk.
—Dr. Jim Will, Psychologist

Do you know what my favorite part of the game is? The opportunity to play. It's as simple as that. God, I love that opportunity.
—Mike Singletary, Football Hall of Famer

Being cold, like being determined to win, is just a state of mind.
—Woody Hayes, Football Coach

The most important coach any athlete will ever have is herself. During a softball game, each athlete has two roles: coach and athlete. A leader coaches herself, and sometimes others, between pitches. When it is time for action, she stops coaching and becomes an athlete.

Self-coaching is a product of self-talk. Self-talk is simply thoughts, the dialogue going on in a person's head. Self-talk is usually in the form of actual words, although it sometimes takes the form of pictures or concepts. Right now, your self-talk is the words you are reading, although if you pause from the text, your mind could venture off in a thousand different directions. Even while you read, you can have distracting self-talk or you can be focused singularly on the task at hand. If athletes could simply not think, their talent would probably flow uninterrupted into their performance, but humans think… a lot. Estimates indicate that the average person has between 25,000 and 75,000 distinct thoughts per day (and scary though it may be, that over half of them are negative).

A softball player has many, many thoughts during the course of a game and those thoughts affect her performance. Just like gravity affects a person who does not understand what it is, these thoughts will impact performance level whether she has awareness or not. The pertinent question is not, "Will I talk to myself?" That answer is set in stone. The question is, "Will my self-talk optimize my performance?" That answer is very much a variable.

Self-talk impacts performance in many ways, including directly affecting attitudes (including confidence), communicating mind to muscle, directing focus, learning skills, making appropriate adjustments, and increasing or decreasing other mental skills such as intensity or toughness/courage. Harvey Dorfman[11] called self-talk the most important mental skill for directly enhancing performance in elite athletes. This chapter will clarify many ways that poor self-talk can keep an athlete from winning the mental side of the game. Personal demons can lead to the following obvious examples of poor self-talk:

- ➢ I'm terrible.
- ➢ This is unbelievable.
- ➢ We have to win.
- ➢ I need to score on this play.

In contrast, the world's greatest athletes think the following phrases right before they perform:

- ➢ This is going to be awesome.
- ➢ I'm ready. Let's do this.
- ➢ I love this game.
- ➢ This is a great opportunity.

---

[11] H. A. Dorfman: author, mental skills coach for too many famous baseball players to count, and mentor to this author. See also: http://www.coachtraub.com/images/A-Tribute-to-Harvey.pdf.

Imitating ideal patterns of self-talk is a sophisticated skill that can be learned. As for any skill, motivation and courage are required.

The gap between good and great is wide. To make the leap, an athlete must do what is difficult – recognize a weakness and build new habits to overcome it. Recognizing and replacing poor patterns of self-talk is tough, but it is also both possible and completely controllable. Once momentum is acquired, the work it takes to traverse the wide gap between good and great may be surprisingly small, especially when compared to the amount of work already put in to become good.

Figure 8-1

Many great athletes maximize use of their talent by working relentlessly on their weaknesses and gearing themselves up to give their best effort every day. Pete Rose has his faults, but his greatness on the diamond is undeniable. "What's tough," Rose said, "is to go out and work hard on the things that you don't do very well." Human nature leads athletes the other way—namely, spending more time practicing the things at which they are already skilled. It is more comfortable and easier this way. The greatness of humanity, however, is that people have the ability to do the unnatural. With effective self-talk, human nature can be overcome, replacing poor patterns of behavior with better ones. Legendary Notre Dame Football Coach Knute Rockne said, "Build up your weaknesses until they become your strengths." With discipline, the unnatural itself can become second nature, or routine.

Playing time often affects the mentality of athletes. Tom Martinez was the quarterback coach for the Green Bay Packers when Aaron Rodgers was backing up Brett Favre. He said, "There are two kinds of guys: the guys who sit and sulk and the guys who sit and gather. Aaron obviously sat and gathered and went out and practiced and got better every day." In fact, he sat for three years before becoming a starter and star performer.

Many people who believe in the value of positive thinking still underestimate the impact that self-talk has on behavior. Thoughts directly affect feelings, which directly affect behaviors. The following exercise will help convince a skeptic.

EXERCISE

First, remember specific times when you had the following thoughts: "I have executed this skill many times before," "This practice is worthless," and "I am being taken advantage of." Second, remember how you felt at those times. Third, remember how you performed in each of these situations. Stop reading now and recall these specifics.

It is likely that you felt confident, impatient, and angry, respectively, and that you performed well, poorly, and poorly, respectively. Ask yourself, "Would different self-talk have likely led to a different level of performance?"

Remember, a primary goal is to figure out what works and repeat it. Leaders recall their own attitude when they gave their greatest performances. With awareness of specifically how they want to feel, their next step is to develop a strategy to consciously program this attitude as part of their pre-practice and pre-game routine.

The tone, not just the content, of self-talk will significantly affect an athlete's attitudes. It is also an indicator of her current state. One good rule of thumb is for the athlete to talk to herself during a game in a manner that she would want her coach to talk to her. Think of the alternative: she would think very little of a coach who calls a time-out to yell criticisms at him in an impatient and frustrated tone. But many athletes talk to themselves in just this manner. Self-coaching should have a dignified and respectful tone, rather than one that is annoyed and demeaning.

Sometimes, the distance of achieving major goals can be a tough obstacle to conquer. The following poem by Wilbur Braithwaite can help athletes and coaches cope with this problem of perspective. Each stanza of the poem is based on a mental skill that will support the pursuit of a major goal: work, steady, fire-up, listen, discipline, patience, defiance, and faith.

Do You Want to be a Champion?

Do you want to run 'til your lungs are tight,
Do you want to hustle with all your might,
Do you want your shirt soaking with sweat,
Work, my son, you'll be a champion yet.

Can you take bad breaks in a hard fought game,
Can you be way down and fight just the same,
Can you face the task with a goal that's set,
Steady, my son, you'll be a champion yet.

Is your spirit inside a burning flame,
Is your want to strong, or feeble and lame,
Is your eye on target, a goal to be met,
Fire-up, young man, you'll be a champion yet.

Do you feel the sting of blisters you've worn,
Do your legs grow limp from bucking the storm,
Do you study odds and know the best bet,
Listen, my son, you'll be a champion yet.

Will you live like a Spartan and always train,
Will you tame your passions for self and the game,
Will you obey the rules that you have set,
Discipline, lad, you'll be a champion yet.

Do you hear voices cry out every mistake,
Do you fear the jeers for errors you make,

Add plus with minus to balance the net,
Patience, my son, you'll be a champion yet.

Can you lose yourself in competitive fire,
Can you lift up your game going down to the wire,
Can you rise from defeat once the verdict is set,
Defiance, my son, you'll be a champion yet.

It's not in the score as much as the mind,
It's not in the glory, the fame, or anything of that kind,
It is in the motto, "You must give to get,"
Hang in there, son, you'll be a champion yet.

EXERCISE

Grade yourself on a scale of 1-100 on how well you do at talking to yourself with dignity and respect, as if talking to a friend, regardless of the circumstances.

_____

The best coaches in the world score 99 or 100 because it is always possible to be critical and respectful at the same time. You are the most important coach you'll ever have. If this exercise brought awareness of room for improvement, that is great news! Get to work, and don't expect to achieve a 99 with good intentions. People are creatures of habit, and a 10% improvement in a week is fantastic.

EXERCISE

To learn more about the mind-body connection, take the following four-second test. In this test, following instructions is important. Take four seconds right now to *not* think of a pink elephant. Simply do not allow the image of a big, bright pink elephant into your head.

Yes is Best

I dwell on what I want to happen, not what I don't want to happen.

Learn to think like a winner… Think positive and visualize your strengths.
—Vic Braden, tennis instructor

A positive attitude and functional self-talk benefit behavior more than many people realize because of the nature of the mind-body connection. On the diamond and off it, many good things result from developing a habit of positive self-talk.

Usually, participants in the pink elephant exercise above will see just what they were trying to avoid in their mind. Exceptions occur only when the request is ignored, the participant is skilled at thinking about nothing (perhaps 5% of athletes), or the participant quickly inserts a positively worded thought into her brain like "think of a blue elephant." Most people see the pink elephant because the word "not" carries no weight in the human mind. "Pink elephant" is the dominant thought, so that image appears, with or without the word "not" in the instructions.

Because humans gravitate towards their most dominant thought, all thoughts by athletes about what not to do should be reframed into positive statements before the performance is attempted (Table 8-1). Obviously, leaders facilitate this for teammates by being and talking positive.

Table 8-1

Negative Statement	Positive Statement with same meaning
Don't press.	Stay within myself.
Don't make a bad throw/pitch.	Throw it through the target.
Don't chase the high rise ball.	See it down or take it.
Don't choke.	Make a play.
Don't hang the change up.	Good, aggressive low strike.
Don't strike out.	Hit the ball.
Don't think too much.	Focus.

One goal of an athlete is to never act while having a negative thought. Pitchers control when the action starts, making this goal somewhat easier for them to achieve. Everyone else reacts to the action. This challenge does not excuse negativism. With practice, an athlete can develop a routine that uses positive instructions and allows her to consistently be in a positive frame of mind when the pitch occurs.

Figure 8-2

If a negative thought presents itself, recognition and a release are called for. The presentation of the negative thought in the mind is not a mistake, nor will it always be avoidable. Indulging in the prolonged continuation of that negative thought is both a mistake and avoidable. Recognition equals awareness, which is a prerequisite for an adjustment. To release, athletes often tell themselves to stop the negative thoughts. This probably will not work unless this idea is accompanied by a new focus on something positive, like what she is trying to do next. The more she practices focusing on her job on the next play, the better she will get at it, but there will be times when the attempt to stop negative thoughts is unsuccessful. When this occurs, there is a single key skill that will allow her to release the negative: forgiveness. When something negative is stuck in the brain, forgive to forget. Forgiveness is an untapped skill for performance enhancement for many highly motivated athletes and it is also critical for happiness in life. Leaders practice this skill just as they do any other.

Common Patterns of Trudging Uphill into the Wind
(Distorted or Irrational Self-Talk)

Sports do not build character. They reveal it.

I may win and I may lose, but I will never be defeated.
—Emmitt Smith, Football Hall of Famer

The following irrational or distorted patterns of self-talk relate in some way to confidence, dealing effectively with pressure, or both. Discouraging these inappropriate patterns does not tacitly accept negative outcomes. Rather, it promotes putting "failure" or competition in a proper perspective and using each experience constructively. The first goal is awareness, thus allowing an adjustment to occur.

Many athletes are relieved when they realize that these poor patterns are not unique to them or even unusual. What is unusual is having the discipline to convert bad habits into new, better ones with a decision to change and diligent, persistent effort.

Oh That Poor, Poor, Super-Talented Kid

The quality of a person's life is in direct proportion to his commitment to excellence, regardless of his chosen field of endeavor.
—Vince Lombardi

Unfortunately, it is extremely common for teenagers and young adults to believe that their self-worth depends on their achievement. Great game or bad game, a leader knows that she is the same person beforehand and afterwards. First, her value as a person does not depend on what happens; as mentioned previously, it is an immeasurable birthright of all humans. Many people feel better when they are reminded (or told for the first time) that they do not have to earn their self-worth.

Augie Garrido, coach of five national championship college baseball teams, specifies self-esteem as the most important factor in the success of his players. Self-worth is a gift, but self-esteem is another story. It must be earned. Superior talent (another gift) typically leads to lots of confidence, especially early in the athletic career. However, it does nothing to build self-esteem. In fact, the athlete with superior talent is often at a disadvantage for building self-esteem because she can get away with poor behaviors and still be "successful" on the diamond for a number of years. Of course, successful is in quotations there because she was merely being "successful" in the way society typically defines it (good statistics, winning). She was not successful as the word is defined in these pages: the peace of mind (high self-esteem) that comes from relentlessly doing her best.

It is useful to know exactly what self-esteem is to help figure out where it comes from. In *The Six Pillars of Self-Esteem*, Dr. Nathaniel Branden says that self-esteem is "a duality of self-efficacy and self-respect". That means it is "the disposition to experience oneself as competent to cope with the basic challenges of life and as worthy of happiness." It can also be thought of, he says, as "the reputation we acquire with ourselves."

Dr. Branden's six pillars, or sources, of self-esteem are living consciously, self-acceptance, self-responsibility, self-assertiveness, living purposefully, and personal integrity. Interestingly, these six pillars correlate closely to Dr. M. Scott Peck's four "tools of suffering" that comprise discipline: delaying gratification, accepting responsibility, dedication to reality, and balancing. Self-esteem is based mostly on controllable variables, including personal integrity, disciplined effort, and kindness, and is also partially based on the uncontrollable variable of the person's upbringing. Integrity is defined as being whole, undivided, or unbroken, like a glass globe without any chips or cracks. To reiterate the thought from earlier in this book, this happens when beliefs, actions, words, and thoughts are all in sync with each other.

The mirror test is the most important test an athlete must pass on her journey. The world may think that she is wonderful or terrible, but it is much more important what she thinks of herself. As told in the poem "The Man in the Glass" by Harry Holland Upchurch, she may fool others, but she will never fool herself, plus she has to live with herself forever. This poem begins:

> When you get what you want in your struggle for self,
> And the world makes you king for a day,
> Just go to the mirror and look at yourself,
> And see what that man has to say.
>
> For it isn't your Father or Mother or wife,
> Whose judgment upon you must pass,
> The fellow whose verdict counts most in your life,
> Is the one staring back from the glass.

He's the fellow to please, never mind all the rest
For he's with you clear to the end
And you have passed your most dangerous test
When the man in the glass is your friend.

Figure 8-3

The Far From Perfect Perfectionist

*I'm not what I ought to be,
Not what I want to be,
Not what I'm going to be,
But I am thankful that I'm better than I used to be.*
—John Wooden

Elite athletes are notorious for being perfectionists. They leave out the last line of that little poem. The idea that perfection is essential is obviously false yet often believed. With perfection expected, the horrible self-coaching that ensues can be debilitating. It is often represented by the bad word "should." Simply replacing this with "could" (e.g. "I could have made that play and would have if I had been at my best") is incredibly healthier.

The degree to which an athlete is a perfectionist is obviously on a sliding scale, but there is a clear pattern that this is more common in female athletes than males. A typical high-level softball team is likely to have one-third to one-half of its players who are extremely hard on themselves. Perfectionists should know that this personality trait is fantastic because it causes them to work hard and pay attention to details. However, it also is a negative when it causes them to snowball their mistakes. This happens, particularly in games, because they beat themselves up and dwell on the past. They lose enthusiasm, confidence, and focus. They need to recognize and adjust by remembering that nobody is perfect, so it makes no sense to expect perfection. Forgive to forget, without settling for mediocrity. This is achieved by striving for perfection, but never expecting it.

Do you know anyone who is perfect? If not, you will probably not be the first, so…

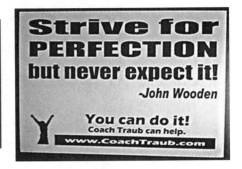

All or Nothing

Outcomes are easy to judge. Too easy.

Polarized thinking is the tendency to view each outcome as an absolute success or an absolute "failure," which is almost never the case. For example, a hitter may miss the hitting the ball on the sweet spot by a millimeter. Despite doing nineteen of twenty things very well, she makes a "loud out" instead of hitting a home run. If the poor outcome is viewed as completely bad, the athlete may fail to repeat all the good things she did, thinking the entire process needs to be changed. If she thinks, "Another fly out? I'm horrible," she may fail to make a subtle adjustment that could lead to a major change in outcomes.

There are an unlimited number of similar examples. Perhaps a pitcher has great movement and velocity, but misses location by six inches. Perhaps the entire team is focused and committed to the plan, but they are not having fun, so they do not fine their ideal state. Leaders consistently gain confidence even through adversity by remembering the good things they did and by making an effective adjustment on their singular mistakes.

Never Say Never

Never lose hope. Dreams do come true. Just believe and never say never.

Related to the all or nothing mentality, athletes tend to overuse the words "never" and "always." Examples: "I always screw up in that situation" or "I can never run a mile in under six minutes." Athletes should avoid these words because they are usually not true. Unfortunately, they are likely to become true if the athlete believes in them. They will return to being false as soon as she ends that belief. Self-fulfilling prophecies are real and common. Almost every athlete has limiting beliefs about herself, and they are just that: beliefs that keep her from approaching her potential.

Of course, exceptions to this rule exist (e.g., never say never). Therefore, every time a competitor is tempted to use an absolute, she should ask the question "Must this be true, or could there be an exception?" If an exception is even remotely possible, she should phrase the idea differently. She can at least change "I'll never do that" into "That's a tough one. *I don't know* if I'll ever be able to do that."

Can't Say Can't

Whether you think you can, or think you can't, you are right.
—Tony Robbins, Motivational Guru

Alone we can do so little; together we can do so much.
—Helen Keller, Deaf and Blind Author and Activist

Positive self-talk doesn't always work, but negative self-talk does.
—Trevor Moawad, Mental Conditioning Coach

History is full of success stories about people who believed they could when conventional wisdom said they could not: man cannot run a mile in under four minutes, man cannot walk on the moon, or a team that barely reached the playoffs cannot win the championship. In professional sports, it is quite common to see the "Wild Card" team win the Super Bowl or World Series. Athletes must be careful not to allow self-fulfilling prophecies to prevent achievement. This often occurs subconsciously and then continues indefinitely because without awareness, no adjustment is possible.

Athletes must also be wary of another, sneaky version of "I can't." "I'm not" means the same thing. Examples of this "yellow light" include "I'm not good enough to compete here," "I'm not tall enough," and "I'm not smart enough." Instead of saying "I'm not," or "we're not," an athlete should express the idea as a challenge. Instead of "We're not going to be able to win this," she can think, "It will be an awesome upset (or comeback) if we pull it off. I'll do my best and see what happens." At the very least, she can say, "I don't know if we can do it."

Figure 8-4

Hate the Word Hate

Forgiveness is the economy of the heart... forgiveness saves the expense of anger, the cost of hatred, the waste of spirits.
—Hannah More, English Religious Writer and Philanthropist

Exceptions exist. Hate is a strong word—usually too strong. Many people use this word carelessly or haphazardly: "I hate running," or "I hate getting out of bed so early." Athletes should say what they mean, even when speaking to themselves. A leader does not "hate" running because she weighs all the positives and negatives honestly. Running leads to improvements in skill and condition, which lead to winning. She loves winning, so even if she finds running tedious, she will not say that she hates it. It is natural to dislike some things (or traits in certain people), but athletes will have more positive energy when they avoid the word "hate."

There's No Crying in Softball (Catastrophizing)

Distance not only gives nostalgia, but perspective, and maybe objectivity.
—Robert Morgan, Poet

Catastrophizing means imagining the worst possible thing that could happen and thinking that this outcome is terrible and would be difficult to ever overcome. This perspective leads to large waves of emotions, rather than the even keel that marks the tough-minded leader. There are no catastrophes in sports, other than a rare severe injury or death. With a proper perspective, no single loss or "failure" will ever be viewed as a catastrophe, because it will have no direct impact on the athlete's identity. The pressure-inducing thought "I need to" is then replaced with the thought, "This is a great opportunity to" or "I would like to."

Brett Favre said, "Football is important but not as important as you once thought it was. When you lose a family member or something tragic happens, that stays with you forever." Baseball relief pitcher and Hall of Famer Goose Gossage said, "Every time I come into a game, I think of my home in the Rockies, and that relaxes me. I tell myself the worst thing that could happen is that I'd be home fishing there tomorrow." Losing is bad, but it is not a catastrophe. Often, asking "What's the worst that could happen" will help an athlete realize that she is catastrophizing and is therefore likely to let her fear negatively impact her behavior.

Figure 8-5

No Fair, No Kidding

*Things tend to turn out best for the people who make the best
of the way things tend to turn out.*

The fallacy of fairness is the idea that life *should* be fair. Thinking or saying, "This is not fair" (or, "Unbelievable" to mean the same thing) is often a disguise for a person wanting her personal preferences versus what someone else thinks is right or best. It leads to an emotional response that interferes with an effective rational response. Thinking that life should be fair is analogous to an athlete banging her head against a brick wall in an attempt to break the wall. It will not work, but it will hurt. Leaders recognize that overcoming obstacles that seem unfair is a necessary step towards success. Plus, they not only recognize that life is not fair, they emotionally accept it -- even embrace it. They make unfair circumstances their challenge rather than their problem. Doing so gives them a competitive edge, and they know it.

It's All My Fault

The worst guilt is to accept an unearned guilt.
Ayn Rand, Author

I don't believe in guilt, I believe in living on impulse as long as you never intentionally hurt another person, and don't judge people in your life. I think you should live completely free.
Angelina Jolie, Actress

Many athletes assume disproportionate guilt, taking too much personal responsibility for a disappointing outcome. The weight of the world will not promote a relaxed peak performance. The idea that any softball player is solely responsible for her team's loss is false and can lead to dangerous conclusions such as "My teammates must hate me" or "I'm worthless." Team games are exactly that—team games. It is easy to focus on the last play in a close game, but keep in mind what John Wooden preached: a free throw in the first minute of the game is of equal value and therefore equal importance to a free throw in the last minute. Like many of Wooden's lessons, this lesson is logical and simple, yet often forgotten.

Balanced Rationality is Bad (Permanence)

Great leaders not only emphasize the good and de-emphasize the bad for themselves, they vocally help their teammates to do it, too.

Permanence, or a one-trial generalization, is the idea that a single outcome is destined to happen over and over. This is actually a fantastic belief when the outcome is good, but horrible self-talk when it is bad. When an athlete executes a play perfectly, she should expect to do so the next time the same situation comes up. A balanced rationality would also expect bad outcomes to repeat, but this is not a useful expectation, nor does it need to be true. An athlete may perform poorly one time in cold weather and decide "I stink when it's cold." This is obviously not the positive, relentless attitude that will lead her to perform up to her potential. The best athletes in the world emphasize one-time good outcomes as likely to happen again, but view a poor outcome as an aberration from the norm. Perfectionists tend to do the opposite, beating themselves up for each mistake and having thoughts like, "Here we go again" or "Today is not my day!"

EXERCISE

The next time the umpire misses a call that works against you, think to yourself:

"Thank you, Mr. Umpire, for providing these adverse circumstances so that I may practice focusing on what I can control and show off my mental toughness skills."

This idea is initially humorous, not because it is a joke, but because it is so far from what is normal. This will work, but if it does not resonate for you, find another thought that does, such as:

"I'm glad he missed that one early on rather than late in the game/at-bat."

or

"If he keeps missing calls like that, it's really going to be a problem for the other team."

Figure 8-6: Even our hero is unable to give a best effort performance with the weight of the world upon her shoulders.

Excuses Are Sneaky

> The man who complains about the way the ball bounces is likely the one who dropped it.
> —Lou Holtz, Football Coach

> Losers never know why they are losing. They will mention injuries, officiating, the weather, and bad breaks.
> —George Allen, Football Coach

As was discussed in Dr. M. Scott Peck's description of discipline in Chapter 3, acceptance of responsibility for personal behavior is critical. When confronted with a dilemma or tough situation, a person either will find a way or find an excuse, but never both. Excuses are like candy at Christmas: abundant but not healthy. As an athlete increases her acceptance that she is completely responsible for and in control of her behavior, which is all that can be controlled, she will develop an intolerance of excuses.

Most excuse makers agree with the preceding paragraph, yet they unwittingly continue to make excuses. These excuses sneak up on them in various forms and often include words or phrases from the poor patterns of self-talk listed above. Perhaps the excuse maker's ego is fragile, needing the protection of excuses. Life will eventually teach her the benefits of accepting responsibility and the pitfalls of fearing "failure," hopefully sooner rather than later. Awareness is the first step because without awareness, no adjustment is possible. Leaders drop their safety net and do their best, one step at a time, regardless of environmental difficulties. No matter what potential excuses exist, she can always do her best.

Frankly, I Do Give a Damn, but...

> Shallow men believe in luck or in circumstance. Strong men believe in cause and effect.
> —Ralph Waldo Emerson, Poet

Personalization of anything bad is the self-defeating tendency to personalize every "failure," without regard to evidence that may indicate that an event has nothing to do with the athlete or was outside of her control. She may fail to give a worthy opponent appropriate credit. She may accept responsibility for a poor outcome when her performance was good, but her luck was bad. She may have disproportionate guilt after a loss. Excuses are bad and accepting responsibility is good, but it is *not* uncommon in softball to take these concepts too far. Leaders seek balance by understanding what they can control and hunting for reasons when outcomes are unacceptable. They do not go into a shell, become inconsolable, or "hate" softball after a loss. They see reality accurately, including when a poor outcome is not their fault. Then they form a best guess about how to make an appropriate adjustment, unless no adjustment is called for which is sometimes the case.

Running Downhill with the Wind (Transforming Self-Talk)

> Listen to yourself. Catch yourself. Change your thoughts, and yourself.
> —H.A. Dorfman, Mental Skills Coach

If an athlete's self-talk is not ideal, then one of three strategies can be used to improve it: countering, reframing, or thought stoppage. Countering is combating a thought with logic and recognizing it as untrue. Reframing is looking at a true idea from a better angle. Thought stoppage means simply focusing on something more useful.

Since every athlete is her own most important coach, it is important that she recognizes when she says things to herself that are not true. Countering is simply gaining this awareness; it fixes the problem.

Table 8-2

Original thought:	Countered thought:
We need to score now.	We can still win even if we don't score this inning.
We need to score now.	We don't have to win this game.
I'm terrible.	I'm not terrible.
This is unbelievable.	This is reality.
I can't.	I can.
The umpire is blind.	The umpire is not blind; he is just not very good.
Coach will hate me if I strike out.	Coach will not hate me if I strike out.
My hard work wasn't worth anything if I don't get a scholarship.	My hard work was worth a lot whether I get a scholarship or not.

If the statement was true, countering is not possible. However, it still may not be a useful thought. Reframing is saying the same thing from a better point of view.

Pressure can be minimized with reframing, or negatives can be turned into positives.

Table 8-3

Original thought:	Reframed thought:
I'm not as good as I want to be.	I'm better than I used to be.
It's bad that the umpire is bad.	It's good that the umpire is bad.
Being a perfectionist is a curse.	Being a perfectionist is a blessing.
My changeup is too inconsistent.	My changeup has a chance to become a dominating pitch.
This field is horrible.	This lousy field will give us an edge. We can handle it better than they can.
We're too far behind.	This is an opportunity for a great comeback.
I'm supposed to lead; I've got to play better.	The game is difficult, but if I give my best effort, things will work out.
Striking out is bad.	Striking out is good. If I didn't ever strike out, I'd be playing competition that was too weak.
It's so hot.	I'm glad it's not raining.
The world is ugly.	The world is beautiful.

Sometimes, it is difficult to figure out a way to counter or reframe an unhelpful thought. Thought stoppage, whereby one line of thought is ended and a new one is begun, makes the appropriate adjustment in these cases. For example, an athlete should stop thinking "I stunk it up last time," release the past by forgiving to forget if that thought is stuck in her head, and refocus on the task at hand.

Ideal self-talk leads to playing the game one play at a time from a trusting attitude. An athlete gets to that wonderful place where a peak performance can happen when her self-talk has already (1) built her ideal attitude for the situation, (2) has committed her to an effective plan of attack, and (3) prepared her to focus entirely on the task at hand. At this point, she is ready to play, not coach herself. She is not worrying about anything and no room exists in her mind for instructions. Some people would refer to this mode as non-thinking, which is fine, though in this trust mode, a thought does exist in the athlete's head. It comes from being engrossed in the game. It is that simple, singular, tunnel-vision focus on the task at hand where awareness of relevant cues is enhanced and no attention is given to irrelevant information from the environment.

Figure 8-7

CHAPTER 9

BUILDING SWAG

> You gotta believe.
> —Tug McGraw, Baseball Hall of Famer

> Confidence is a very fragile thing.
> —Joe Montana, Football Hall of Famer

> When anyone tells me I can't do anything… I'm just not listening anymore.
> —Florence Griffith-Joyner, Track Olympian

> Besides pride, loyalty, discipline, heart, and mind, confidence is the key to all the locks.
> —Joe Paterno, Football Coach

Confidence (swag, swagger) level correlates highly with performance level. Great performers trust their skills and believe that things will go well. Muhammad Ali said, "I am the greatest. I said that even before I knew I was." It is a valuable pursuit to figure out how to obtain and maintain a high confidence level before and during a game. Unfortunately, it is a common misconception that a person either has confidence or she does not. In fact, confidence is an attitude and attitudes are controllable. Leaders imitate the thinking patterns of the greatest athletes in the world.

Confidence comes from preparation, self-esteem, and one other significant factor. Most people think this other factor is past experiences. Actually, confidence comes from the way people think about the experiences they have had. This distinction is subtle, but huge because the past is not controllable, but the way athletes think about the past is completely controllable. Once it is time to perform, preparation and self-esteem are constants. However, an athlete's confidence in her ability to execute this next play is very much a variable. Preparation (Chapter 13) and self-esteem are discussed in other parts of this book. This chapter focuses on how to use self-talk to consciously increase confidence right now.

Many athletes have never thought about this subtle distinction that confidence fluctuates not based on experiences, but on the way they think about these experiences. Therefore, they typically emphasize their most recent experiences. This is a natural pattern of self-talk. When they do this, the belief that confidence comes from experiences becomes true. It is a self-fulfilling prophecy that is fine when recent experiences are good, but very damaging when recent experiences are bad.

Did Cat Osterman lose confidence after giving up a hit? Did Jessica Mendoza lose confidence if her first at-bat of a game was a strikeout? Do any of the greatest athletes in the world allow their confidence to suffer because of a single mistake or episode of bad luck? Of course not. They use the experience to learn, and then they flush the past from their minds. Since they were already good and now they learned more, their confidence rises, even after a mistake. If needed, they lean on thoughts about past peak performances to consciously build their confidence. Recall that if Michael Jordan missed his first five shots, he thought back to a game where he missed his first five and made his next ten.

Since confidence is largely the direct result of particular thinking habits, making the commitment to consciously gain confidence by using effective patterns of self-talk is a top priority for leaders. These patterns allow athletes to hang on to and thus benefit from successful experiences and let go of, or de-emphasize, less successful experiences. This unbalanced relationship of emphasizing positives and de-emphasizing negatives is the secret to consciously increasing confidence. It is called an optimistic explanatory style.

A leader's job = Give her team her best effort and help her teammates to do the same.

Best effort requires a confident attitude.

Attitudes come from thoughts.

CONCLUSION:

A big part of a leader's job is to think in patterns that maximize her own confidence.

Good is Good; Bad is Good (Optimistic Explanatory Style)

> If we magnified blessings as much as we magnify disappointments,
> we would all be much happier.
> —John Wooden

> What I represent is just achieving what you want to do in life. It's a matter of your attitude.
> Some people have a negative attitude, and that's their disability.
> —Marla Runyan, first legally blind athlete to compete in the Olympic Games

Every athlete should ask herself if her glass is half full or half empty. Pessimistically, it is half empty. Realistically, it is both; things could always be better and they could always be worse. Leaders optimistically think of it as half full. It is simply more useful to be positive. Consistent winners either have or are learning to have an optimistic explanatory style of self-talk. They emphasize positives and de-emphasize negatives.

Unfortunately, many talented performers who have not been exposed to any mental skills training have a personality that pulls their thoughts in the exact opposite direction. Their high standards cause them to emphasize every little mistake and gloss over all the positive things they are doing. This perfectionist tendency helps motivate them to prepare thoroughly, which is great. Unfortunately, it also erodes their current level of confidence. Therefore, their goal should be to emphasize what comes naturally to them when it is useful (typically, when it is time to train) and consciously change what is being emphasized in their minds when it is harmful (typically, when it is time to perform). With awareness and practice, this is not difficult, but without awareness, no adjustment is possible.

Suppose a pitcher is a perfectionist. She is the hardest worker on the team. She prepares diligently from the weight room to practice to strategy with the scouting report. Then she gets in the game and is playing well until she makes one mistake. Perhaps she tried a little too hard and lost her rhythm or mechanics. Or maybe she throws to the wrong base or walks the nine-hole batter. Perhaps she even does everything correctly, but a bad hop leads to a run and she blames herself.

There are infinite pitfalls for a perfectionist. This athlete, who is so close to being a great leader, starts beating herself up. She emphasizes in her self-talk how terrible she must be to allow such a mistake to happen. Her confidence suffers, her performance suffers, and her leadership suffers. She lacks the consistency and mental toughness needed to be great.

Many athletes who struggle with consistency think with some measure of this perfectionist pattern. They have no even keel and no strategies for consciously building confidence. When tough sledding hits, they allow their recent experiences to pull them down, magnifying the problem rather than overcoming it.

An example of an athlete with an optimistic explanatory style comes from a true story about a basketball player. Stuart was a senior who led his team in scoring and shot 50% from the field. In a high school playoff game, he was 0 for 16 shooting, but his team was down by only one point when it got a steal with time running out. During the ensuing time-out, the coach logically called a play for someone else. Stuart saw that his teammate was scared. The coach saw it, too and began to panic for a lack of options, but Stuart said, "Give me the ball. I'll make it." The coach reluctantly agreed. Stuart's team got him the ball near the free-throw line. Stuart eyed the target and confidently let it fly for the game winner. Interestingly, for making just one shot that day, Stuart was called a hero.

Afterwards, this story was told and someone asked Stuart how he had the confidence to want that shot when he was 0 for 16 on the day. "I'm a 50% shooter," he said, "so when I miss the first shot, I figure I'm due to make the next one. When I miss two, I'm overdue. At 0 for whatever, I just knew the next one had to go in!" That is a shooter's mentality! The evidence was undeniable: Stuart was so confident that he requested the ball. Next he was asked, "What do you think if you start out a game 3 for 3 from the field? Are you likely to miss the next shot because you're a 50% shooter?" Stuart replied, "Of course not. If I'm on fire, give me the ball!" "You can't have it both ways," came the reply. "Of course you can," said Stuart, wise beyond his years. This is precisely how great athletes think. Interestingly, this high school multi-sport star, Stuart Anderson, went on to play football in the NFL.

This story illustrates the positively unbalanced relationship of self-talk that defines an optimistic explanatory style. Good stuff is good. Bad stuff is not only bad, it is also good. This could be considered a means of tricking oneself solely to increase confidence. This trickiness is not only fair, it is necessary to maximize confidence and, therefore, performance.

An optimistic explanatory style can occur in three specific ways: permanence, pervasiveness, and personalization. Permanence is the likelihood that something occurring once will happen again. Pervasiveness refers to the likelihood that an outcome (or controllable result) in one area will lead to a similar outcome in a different area. Personalization refers to an event being caused by a person's own behavior. With the suggested patterns of thinking, an athlete explains (emphasizes) a *positive* experience by saying to herself that the good result is likely to occur consistently (permanence), across domains (pervasiveness), or is because of her own behavior (personalization). Or all three. A *negative* experience is explained (de-emphasized) as being a deviation from the norm (permanence), representative of an event in that area only (pervasiveness), or the outcome of uncontrollable factors outside of her control (personalization). Or all three.

Denying responsibility sounds very similar to making an excuse. Sometimes that is exactly what it is, but sometimes it is a reason rather than an excuse. Intolerance for excuses is superb. However, every time an athlete accepts responsibility for a negative outcome, her confidence takes a hit. Denying responsibility for a negative outcome will prevent damage to her confidence. This denial is always appropriate if it is true! For example, an infielder may play the ground ball correctly, but get an error when the ball takes an unpredictable, bad hop.

Athletes who focus on controllable behavior will have no trouble recognizing when a poor outcome follows good behavior, but those athletes who focus solely on outcomes often forget to analyze behavior by trying to accept responsibility for all outcomes. They mistakenly think that accepting responsibility for everything demonstrates maturity.

Denying personal responsibility for an outcome is often appropriate even if it only *might* be true that the behavior did not cause the outcome. Sometimes the athlete simply will not know. If finding a conclusion about responsibility is not immediately possible, denying responsibility for a poor outcome will benefit her confidence. Of course, it might also prevent a useful adjustment, so a best guess is required. One rule of thumb is to deny responsibility for negative outcomes during games to keep confidence high but accept it after the game or in practice to promote learning. On the other side of the coin, an athlete should believe that a good outcome during a game is because of her, even if she is unsure.

For example, a pitcher may be called for an illegal pitch. Perhaps she should do something different, but she may not be able to know the answer to that question until she gets to look at the videotape with a coach. If the illegal pitch was only called one time, it is useful for her to deny responsibility for the mistake for now to prevent damage to her confidence. (This is a fine line to walk. Teammates are suggesting this thinking pattern when they tell the pitcher that it was a bad call. This is great for confidence, but horrible for making adjustments, so if an immediate adjustment is needed, it would obviously not be the right time for this pattern of thinking.)

Examples of an Optimistic Explanatory Style

In each example, the athlete's self-talk allows her confidence level to increase after a good outcome, or prevents it from decreasing after a poor outcome.

Situation #1: A catch or missed catch on a tough play for the outfielder.

Emphasizing the Good

Permanence: I made a good catch and if I get another chance, I'll make another good catch.
Personalization: I made that good catch because I've got great hands.
Pervasiveness: I made that good catch because I'm a great ball player. Therefore, I'll probably hit well, too.

De-emphasizing the Bad

Permanence: I didn't make that good catch, but I usually do catch those so that was just a one-time thing.
Personalization: I didn't make that catch because my teammate didn't communicate with me. Had I known that it was my ball, I would've caught it.
Pervasiveness: I didn't make that good catch, but that has nothing to do with my ability to hit, so I'm still likely to have a quality at-bat.

Situation #2: An RBI or missed opportunity when batting with a runner on third base and one out.

Emphasizing the Good

Permanence: I drove in that run and will do it again.
Personalization: The reason I was able to make positive contact to the outfield is because I had a good, aggressive plan, saw it well, got a good pitch to hit, and put a good swing on it.
Pervasiveness: I'm an RBI machine and I can help us win games on defense, too.

De-emphasizing the Bad

Permanence: I didn't get the run in, but that just means I'm due for a good at-bat next time I'm in that situation.
Personalization: I know this umpire's zone, and if he hadn't widened it on the first pitch, I wouldn't have swung at the 0-1 pitch that was also outside, the one that I hit a weak grounder on.
Pervasiveness: I didn't get that run in, so I'll go help us win on defense.

An athlete can actually learn from a mistake and then de-emphasize it with the overall thought pattern strategy of emphasizing positives and de-emphasizing negatives. For example, a hitter could de-emphasize a strikeout by thinking, "I learned that this pitcher will try to get ahead in the count with curve balls and expand the strike zone with two strikes up and down with the rise ball and changeup, respectively. I will use this knowledge to form a better plan of attack next at-bat.

Derek Jeter, New York Yankee shortstop and future Hall of Famer, had no hits in 32 straight at-bats during one stretch early in the 2004 season. Following is a quote that explains Jeter's optimistic explanatory style:

> *You should always think you are going to be successful and you should always want to be successful. If it doesn't work out... acknowledge that something went wrong, adjust your actions and go after it again the next time. The next time you try that task, don't think about the time you faltered. Think about all of the times in which you have excelled. That's a path back to success.*

Jeter hit .293 with 23 home runs and a career high 44 doubles in 2004.

Staying Unstuck on the Fast Track Up

The best teams try to fix things when they're winning, not after they start to lose.
—Kevin Constantine, NHL Coach

Success is one of the biggest preventers of growth. People think 'don't screw it up.' So they don't change, and somebody else leaps ahead of them.
—Doug Hall, Author

People say you learn from losing, but I think you can learn just as well from winning.
—John Wooden

Discipline and diligence are up there on the list, but one of the most important qualities of many really successful people is humility. If you have a degree of humility about you, you have the ability to take advice, to be coachable, teachable.
A humble person never stops learning.
—Todd Blackledge, NFL quarterback

Difficulties in life are intended to make us better, not bitter.
—Dan Reeves, Football Coach

Disappointment and "failures" are not bad things. To appreciate this concept, it is useful to understand the outcomes curve and the knowledge curve. In some sport psychology textbooks, this idea is represented by curves called performance and learning (Figure 9-3). From a distance, the performance and learning curves have the same general shape: sharp increases at the beginning of learning a skill, eventually leveling off as a person approaches her potential much later. Viewed up close, the curves are quite different. The performance curve has ups, downs, and plateaus. The learning curve, however, looks the same up close as it does from a distance. It is smooth because learning never goes down. When outcomes temporarily decline, learning can still occur.

Figure 9-1

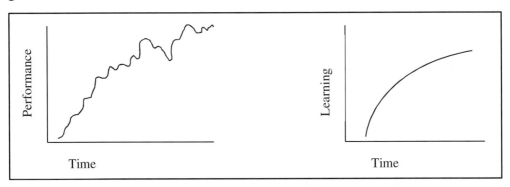

Normally, emotions flow with the outcomes curve. When outcomes are good, the athlete is pleased and vice versa. The point of these two curves is to show that emotions do not have to decline when an athlete has a rough day of performance. She can choose to focus on learning rather than outcomes. Learning, which in the long run is more important than one day's performance, is still going up. Athletes should not fear "failure." Rather, they should welcome mistakes (especially aggressive ones) because they promote learning.

This primary point about keeping a positive attitude through adversity is wonderful. However, some adjustments to the curves (shown in Figure 9-5) make them even more accurate and useful. The concepts are similar, but the new labels, shapes, and explanations provide useful distinctions. The first difference is the y-axis labels. Performance can be good while an outcome is poor. The concept being referred to in the performance curve is outcomes, not just the controllable behavior that the word "performance" implies. The shape of this curve stays the same. In the learning curve, the knowledge that results from learning is what is actually being charted. A true learning "curve" as described by the shape of the knowledge level being charted in Figure 9-3 would be a horizontal line: consistent progress forward at a constant rate.

Figure 9-2

Figure 9-3

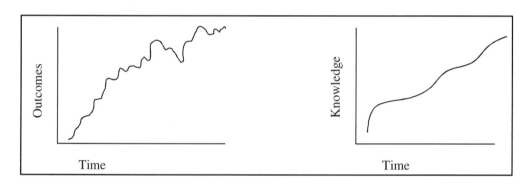

Learning, however, is not a constant. The knowledge curve in Figure 9-5 looks somewhat like a set of waves on a slope, with that horizontal line as its average. The different labels on the curves in Figures 9-3 and 9-5 are primarily differences of semantics, but the critical point is *how* the rate of learning fluctuates. It is not a function of outcomes at all but rather a function of the athlete's attitude and environment. Learning is not always happening, as the curve in Figure 9-3 suggests. Knowledge does not increase without intelligent effort. It is true that students with a poor attitude do not get dumber, but they do not get smarter either. Some athletes do not learn after a poor outcome because they are too upset to pay attention and have an effective rational response. Some athletes do not learn after good outcomes because they are satisfied. Many athletes have simply developed a habit of mental laziness instead of alertness. Some do not learn as fast because they are not in as challenging an environment as others. Their competition is lower and their chances to compete under championship conditions are few and far between. As Coach Wooden said, "Do not mistake activity for achievement." Leaders always try to figure out what works and repeat it and what does not work so that they can change it. They find a way to consistently learn, fast.

It is normal to allow negative emotions to follow negative outcomes, but a coach or athlete would not be reading these words if normalcy was her goal. Ideally, athletes always seek to improve as fast as possible, and they are pleased with all outcomes as long as their effort and progress are high. They know that both good and poor outcomes are part of the process of approaching their potential, and their rate of learning is the most important determinant of success.

Figure 9-4

With an understanding of the knowledge curve and an optimistic explanatory style, it is clear that mistakes do not inevitably destroy confidence. Instead, mistakes can be viewed as necessary steps of progress. Unfortunately, most athletes lose confidence as they gain experience because they selectively attend more to the emotions that accompany these inevitable mistakes than to the progress being made. They become more cautious, tentative, and fearful as they advance to higher levels of play. On the other hand, some athletes build confidence despite repeated "failures" because they selectively attend to every small improvement and positive experience that occurs. The following Derek Jeter quote shows why he is an exemplar:

> *"If you can remember one or two positives from your pursuit of a certain goal, you'll begin each day with confidence. It's hard to overlook mistakes, and we shouldn't ignore them because we can learn from them. But when you're really toiling, you need to find those shreds of optimism and cling to them."*

Champions are Coachable

"Once the person commits to being coached, s/he begins to experience a different, more hopeful world as his or her perceptions evolve."
—John G Agno, Leadership Coach and Author

Coaches often suggest (or demand) an adjustment. They believe that the proposed change will help avoid future disappointing outcomes. Because of their experience, they are able to anticipate a problem and suggest the solution. Usually, the athlete would not seek this solution on her own until she struggles with outcomes. If the adjustment is to be made either now or later, it is better to make it now, before the bad outcome happens. On the other hand, it is reasonable to think twice before changing what currently seems to be working. Balance is required. Every athlete should use rational thought (not ego-driven emotions) and trusted sources of information to make her decision about her best course of action.

Every athlete is the most important coach she will ever have and both strategy and mechanical development are ultimately her decisions to make. It is certainly useful to be courageous about trying new things. A leader is never completely satisfied with the status quo. Her eagerness to learn is defined by these traits: approachable, attentive, curious, trusting, and confident. She lacks arrogance and defensiveness; rather, she is inquisitive by nature. Learning faster than her competition today is her top goal, because she knows this means more winning in the future. Therefore, she is grateful when someone else might be able to help her achieve this goal faster than she could on her own. She listens with the intent to learn, not the intent to be right or smart. When something does not work, she searches for the reasons within herself rather than making the excuse of blaming others.

Figure 9-5

The coachable athlete demonstrates leadership in many different ways. Her body language communicates gratitude and enthusiasm to herself and others. She sits up and makes eye contact when the coach addresses the team. She nods her head when she hears a good idea and she is not afraid to try new things. She knows that not every new idea will work for her, but she tries the adjustment with optimism that once she gets a little comfort and familiarity with it, this will make her better. Her eagerness for improvement is contagious; her presence helps the attitude of both her teammates and her coaches. As a result, she and her team get better, faster.

Coaches sometimes suggest adjustments that initially seem pointless, strange, or impossible. Perhaps the coach's opinion that the new way will be better is wrong, but perhaps the athlete does not yet understand enough about herself or the game to completely understand the coach's request. She should keep an open mind and do it right, which is to execute the request as best she can, *and* with positive expectations. If she does what the coach told her with the attitude reflected by the thought, "this is a lousy idea," she is creating a self-fulfilling prophecy. She will prove herself right, missing an opportunity to grow in the process. With an optimistic attitude, difficulties, triumphs, struggles, and growth become normal parts of the process by thinking of each task as a skirmish in the war to mold herself into a champion. She is hopeful that the new way is better, even when her current opinion is that her old way is better. What is right is important; who is right has no importance. With a good attitude and superior effort, success is assured.

Figure 9-6

Anything new will feel awkward for a while. Initially feeling weird does not, in itself, make something wrong (although comfort is certainly important in the long run). A coach has been given authority for a reason. Hopefully, it was a good reason. This person may have studied the details of what is going on for years, doing it him- or herself, discussing options with colleagues, and working with other athletes who have already dealt with similar issues. The athlete should be open to the possibility that her coach's judgment is better than her own at this point in time. This openness is called being "coachable," and it is high praise.

Dump the Slump

> You must accept your disappointments and triumphs equally.
> —Harvey Penick, Golf Coach

> The first thing I do after losing is forget it.
> —Nancy Lopez, Golf Hall of Famer

Neither behavior nor outcomes are constants. Therefore, trends of successful outcomes and trends of "failures" are inevitable. Quote marks for "failure" and "slump" remind athletes that these words are not correct, thus de-emphasizing the negatives.

When times are tough, a leader's thinking pattern expects improvement. If an athlete does not believe in the "slump," it does not exist. She may be struggling, scuffling, unlucky, and even frustrated, but she is not "slumping." Slumps are real. "Slumps" are not. A "slump" is simply a recent decline in performance. It happens. An athlete should not validate a "slump" into a slump, which would mean that continued struggles are expected and likely. Outcomes will go up, down, and stay about the same. When they go down for a while, other people will label that trend a slump. A smart athlete, however, does not fall into that trap because she understands that by believing in a slump, she makes it real. The last thing she wants is a self-fulfilling prophecy that saps her confidence, magnifies problems, and anticipates rocky roads ahead. (Another sneaky version of this: "today is not my day.") Her recently poor outcomes are simply an inevitable part of the process of approaching her potential. Instead of validating her "slump," she believes that she is overdue. Overdue and slumping report the same past. The difference is in the athlete's expectations.

If the equation of an optimistic explanatory style was balanced, quotes would be used for successes, too. This would indicate that trends are just things of the past; they do not predict the future. But a self-fulfilling prophecy that says "I am doing my job well and expect that to continue" is useful. This is the unbalanced rationality of athletes who build their confidence through their self-talk.

Slumps (sans quotes) can debilitate a well-meaning, hard-working athlete. When deep in a slump, an athlete "knows" that something significant must be wrong, so she looks for and tries almost any adjustment she can find. Major changes are an option and perhaps a necessity. On the other hand, if others say she is "slumping" and she disagrees, she is demonstrating an understanding of the normalcy of this tough period. She knows that while things have not gone her way lately, she is still doing many things right. Therefore, she will look for subtle adjustments that might help her get back to her normal level of performance, or higher. Sometimes no adjustment at all is needed, or perhaps only a mental adjustment is needed, not a physical one. Often, for example, the "slumping" athlete is pressing, especially if she is not using those quote marks. Perhaps all she needs to do is relax and see the ball well. Sometimes, one "little" tweak to mechanics will make a huge difference. Whatever the case, she will not lose major parts of her confidence by validating the "slump" into a slump.

Figure 9-7

Elite Athlete Audio #3 –Confidence is a synopsis of this chapter. Use your QR Code Reader to listen in a web browser.
    Coach Traub's EAAs = *Crisp. Convenient. Inspirational.*

Putting the Egg Before the Chicken
(Confidence Precedes Greatness)

I will give my best effort one play at a time.

I will prepare and someday my chance will come.
—Abraham Lincoln, President

A man is always better than he thinks he is.
—Woody Hayes, Football Coach
If my mind can conceive it, and my heart can believe it, I know I can achieve it.
—Jesse Jackson, Civil Rights Leader

Confidence comes not from always being right, but from not fearing to be wrong.
—Peter McIntyre, Author

In the age-old argument about which came first, the chicken or the egg, no definitive answer can be found. Many people think the same way about confidence and successful outcomes. One leads to the other and vice versa. But knowledge of the sources of confidence reveals an actual answer: those individuals who think most effectively consciously enhance their confidence and self-trust, even before successful outcomes occur. If an athlete wants to succeed in a new venture, she should maximize her chances by performing with confidence. Whether it is her first varsity game, her first postseason opportunity, or her first time facing an opponent with a fine reputation, she can approach her performance with confidence by thinking with an optimistic explanatory style. This includes emphasizing the parts of this new situation that are familiar, such as a pitcher's routine and goal for each pitch (to hit a spot, aggressively). Confidence does not guarantee her a good performance, of course, but it does increase her chances. Control the controllables.

Power phrases, or affirmations, are simple, positive, self-directed thoughts such as, "I am a smart and strong hitter." They are a form of mental practice that can be used away from the diamond, in practice, or during games. They are reminders of past successes, personal strengths, or positive expectations that an athlete gives herself to increase her confidence. They are used anytime an athlete says simple positive statements to herself, often repetitively. Two-time Olympian Sean O'Neill made power phrases a standard five-minute part of his pre-match routine. He would simply sit and remind himself of all the great things he can do and the things he has accomplished: "I have the best forehand in the world," "If I stay focused, I will win," "I am the national champion," and so on.

Figure 9-8

Power phrases may seem a bit tautological and effusive, but if they improve performance, then they have value. They are like the statements a great coach would make to an athlete at just the time she needs to hear it to maximize her confidence. Since she is the most important coach she will ever have, and the most reliable, she can benefit by systematically using power phrases during her pre-performance routines. This is particularly valuable for the athletic personality which tends to get stuck thinking about negatives. Every athlete/scientist should put power phrases into her experimental design to see if they help.

Figure 9-9

Athletes who understand the way that their confidence fluctuates know that with practice, having a feeling of confidence when it is time to perform is something they can control. Experiences and family history are factors, but pre-performance routines and their patterns of thought are more important. Great athletes use both positive and negative experiences to build their confident attitude. They build their global confidence (self-esteem) by working hard and smart. This prepares them physically and mentally. Finally, their self-talk includes an optimistic explanatory style that emphasizes useful thoughts and de-emphasizes the ones that would hurt confidence.

Athletes' Power Phrases

I am a smart and strong player.
I give my best effort and accept whatever happens.
I play the game one pitch at a time.
My best effort is always good enough.
I am confident because I am prepared.
I am talented and excited to play today.
I trust my teammates and my ability.
I am seeing the ball big.
I am fast and focused.
I am [insert desired trait].
I have a great screwball.
I have a great [insert skill].
I am in control before each pitch.
I am confident and decisive.
I use enthusiasm to do special things.
I hold myself and others in high regard.
I can handle any adversity that comes my way.
I act based on my plan, not in reaction to things outside of my control.
I always play aggressively and under control.
By my aggressive approach, I create magical moments. I enjoy training.
I enjoy training.
I am a lean, mean machine.
I relentlessly do my job for my team.
I prepare so that I may move with poise and confidence.
I thrive under pressure.
I love softball and the challenges it provides.

More Athletes' Power Phrases

I constantly strive for perfection.

I never expect perfection of myself or others

We are raising the bar and I am holding myself accountable.

Every day and in every way, I am getting better and better.

I work hard and deserve the wealth, beauty, and love that is all around me.

I am grateful that I can expand my horizons simply by doing one thing that is outside of my familiar zone today.

I trust my instincts and my closest friends.

I have patience and faith that my dreams will find me if I do my best today.

I always bounce back better than I was when I fell down.

I avoid self-pity and am blessed in many, many ways

With awareness and discipline, I turn weaknesses into strengths.

I keep my head when others are losing theirs.

I am the kind of player whose teammates want up to bat with the game on the line.

I know how to focus and slow the game down.

We are a championship-type of team.

We nip problems in the bud.

When I disagree with someone, I get curious rather than mad.

I intentionally make my attitude worth catching.

Softball is fun, even when it is difficult.

I inspire confidence in others.

When the going gets tough, I lead by example.

Because I care enough to give my best effort at practice, I both deserve and take advantage of every opportunity I get.

When pressure and great opportunities arise, I just do what I do.

Chapter 10

Hyped to the Max (Controlling Performance Anxiety)

I had no chance of controlling a ball game until I first controlled myself.
—Carl Hubbell, Baseball Hall of Fame Pitcher

If you don't have butterflies, it's because you know you have no chance.
—Paul Azinger, Golfer

I get nervous with every shot.
—Tiger Woods, Golfer

The key to success and happiness is to find a middle level.
—Sam Rutigliano, Football Coach

The key to winning is poise under stress.
—Paul Brown, Football Coach

Every game is an opportunity to measure yourself against your own potential.
—Bud Wilkinson, Football Coach

If you can meet triumph and disaster and treat those impostors just the same…
you'll be a man.
—Rudyard Kipling, Poet, from the poem "If"

Attitude is important. If athletes do not get their mind right, they will not give their best effort. However, attitude is just part of the equation for getting ready to perform and learn. Physiology is another key component. Human bodies can do ridiculously amazing things, but they can also be quite clumsy. When an athlete has the best possible internal environment both in her mind and her body, she has achieved one of the requirements for a best effort performance: an ideal state.

The biggest factor in getting the body ready to go can be labeled and measured. It is called hype or arousal level. It refers to how interested, excited, intense, aggressive, and nervous an athlete is. The lowest hype level is physically being in a state of sleep, and the highest level would be a state of wild, raging fury. Hype level affects many variables in an athlete's physiology including her breathing, adrenaline, heart rate, stroke volume and direction of blood flow, muscle tension (including posture), perspiration, and vision. It can also affect many variables in an athlete's mental game, including her focus, perception of time, confidence, attitude, and rhythm.

It is useful to think of a dial from 0 (asleep) to 10 (think Tasmanian Devil) to measure how hyped up an athlete is. Part of a leader's job is to find that spot on the dial where she performs her best for each particular task. If her hype level is too high, she will lack the control needed to execute properly; if it is too low, she will lack energy, aggressiveness, and intensity. Two people can have different ideal hype levels for the same task, just as one person can have two different optimal levels for two different tasks. Most athletes perform most fine motor skill tasks best with a hype number between five and seven.

Figure 10-1 – Hype Level Scale

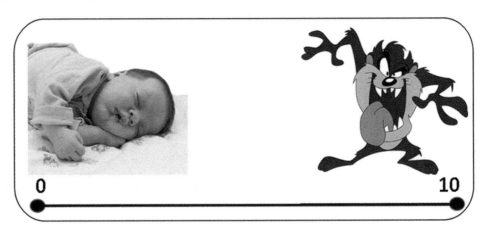

It is the athlete's challenge to get to her optimal arousal level for the task at hand. Many athletes with limited awareness and discipline give their best effort only when their arousal happens to be near its optimal level. Their performance is dependent on their environment. Superior skill in the mental game takes uncontrollables out of the equation as much as possible. Great athletes know how to prepare; they know how to get themselves close to their ideal performance state. Whether in a "clutch" or "routine" situation, the ability to "set the stage" by controlling hype level significantly impacts all athletes' consistency.

Self-control is challenging because many factors outside of an athlete's control can push her hype level too high or too low. She must remember that she has little control of what goes on around her, but total control of how she chooses to respond to what happens. This same concept can be thought of in a different way: between something happening and her responding to it, a space exists. In that space lays her power to choose her response. The quality of her choice will determine what state she is in for what's next, and this will, in turn, determine how fast she learns and how well she performs. The great news about habits is that the more she uses this space (her personal power), the easier it gets to use it again.

Awareness is the foundation skill that allows for effective adjustments; it involves knowing her signals and remembering to check them shortly before performing. To know her "red light," "yellow light," and "green light" indicators, she must pay special attention to this issue of how hyped she is by including physiological and mental variables as key "traffic light" indicators. While learning strategies to "dial it up" or "dial it down," she should use the same strategy that she uses with all mental skills: do what works and discard the rest.

Figure 10-2

Leaders often "dial it up" to avoid missing opportunities. Many athletes have less than stimulating performances because the situation is less than stimulating. To win the mental side of the game, a competitor must recognize when she is feeling bored, apathetic, or overconfident and notice if she is acting lazy. When this happens, she can give herself a pep talk and act better. Why is what she is about to do important? First, to develop the habit of consistently doing things right. Second, she might impress somebody, improve her statistics, or secure her status as a mentally tough performer. Importantly, she might avoid losing a contest that she could win. Acting as if winning is important will soon cease to be an act!

In addition to a pep talk, many strategies exist to "dial it up." Physical motion helps, so an athlete can move around at a speed that represents the level she wants. Imagery can create positive energy. She can try imaging the way her idol plays the game or see herself making a great play. An anchor could quickly end her doldrums (Chapter 16 explains anchoring). Consistently and appropriately using one or more of these strategies will turn any athlete into a coach's favorite: one who lifts up herself and her teammates.

Many athletes get too "hyped up" when performing, particularly in situations they perceive to be more important than others. It is a commonly heard phrase that mentally tough athletes "know how to be comfortable being uncomfortable." This phrase makes no sense, but the concept is correct: tough athletes know how to be comfortable in a situation that would make most people uncomfortable. Every athlete gets nervous at some point. Butterflies start dancing around in stomachs, and the game seems to move faster than normal. In this situation, tough competitors "dial it down" to regain self-control and slow the game down.

The single most effective tool for "dialing it down" is a healthy perspective that says, "My best effort is always good enough. This performance is certainly important, but no situation has a special goal for me because I always strive to do my best." Leaders consciously change their focus from a threat of inadequacy into an opportunity for greatness can, thereby helping dancing stomach butterflies to fly in formation. Confidence certainly helps this change to occur, too. Instead of allowing themselves to think about negative outcomes, leaders think about positive behaviors and positive outcomes. Even the fear of "failure" can be viewed as a positive, since it motivates athletes to behave in a way that will give them the best chance to avoid what it is they fear. Plus, it will keep hype level from being too low.

Figure 10-3

Nervousness often causes an athlete to rush. An athlete can "dial it down" with deep breathing and soothing self-talk that builds confidence. "Nice and easy," she might think in a relaxed tone. "All that matters here is giving my best effort. I know exactly what to do. Just trust it and let it happen." Her routine is also comforting, as it gives him something familiar to lean on, even in a new, potentially uncomfortable environment. An anchor can trigger instant self-control, or imagery might help her slow the game down.

Consistent performers can find the words and images that best bring in and get out the ideas listed in the exercise above. For example, rather than saying "be confident" during the first inhale, picture a personal past peak performance (P.P.P.P.) or use a power phrase to consciously build confidence. Enjoyment reflects not only having fun, but also being fully present in the moment. Exhaling worries is releasing both worries about the future and regrets about the past. Some athletes prefer separating these two with an extra breath.

Having self-control at a hype level of eight is better than having self-control at a level of six. More "juice" is better as long as it is controlled. As an athlete gains mastery over her body, her optimal performance level can rise, but this will not happen without practice. She must take this one step at a time, typically by first learning to calm herself down to a level that she can completely control. With alertness and practice, she will understand how to maintain her balance even with an adrenaline rush, and she will be able to slow the game down even as her heart rate increases.

EXERCISE

Dialing your hype number down:

Breathe deeply, getting the air down towards the belly. Breathe smooth and steady, trying to connect the breaths (smooth out the transitions).

Inhale confidence	Inhale relaxation	Inhale enjoyment
Exhale negativity	Exhale stress	Exhale worries
		(Inhale confidence)

Long Version:
Do each pair 5 times (5 breaths)
Then do each pair 3 times
Then do each pair once
Finish by inhaling confidence one more time

Short version (used during competition):
Do one breath for each.

Practice the long version to increase the impact of the short version.

Comfort affects hype level. Comfortable athletes are relaxed and perform better than uncomfortable, tight athletes. Focusing on the familiar increases comfort while focusing on what is new decreases comfort. This is why a pre-performance routine that is always available is so valuable. Experience is another big factor because it leads to familiarity. The correlation between nerves and comfort is one reason why teams often perform better at home. They are comfortable with the familiar environment, while their opponents are uncomfortable.

Self-esteem also has a great impact on an athlete's ability to control her physiology in tough circumstances. Leaders focus on familiar elements in their job, their environment, and themselves. This allows them to stay relaxed and confident, regardless of the situation. They understand that their best effort is always good enough and that they can know they are giving their best effort, rather than just trying hard, if they prepare and execute their performance routines with discipline.
If an athlete does not have much experience performing under particular conditions (e.g., a new site, the playoffs, a higher level of play following a promotion, and "clutch" late-game situations), she can still excel. It is fine to acknowledge that her lack of experience is a small disadvantage because of the awareness that she has not yet gained. Nevertheless, the game and her job in it are familiar, so she does what she knows: she creates her ideal performance state, commits to an effective plan of attack, and focuses completely on the task at hand.

Experience in postseason play is popular among coaches. People who have "been there before" know what it takes to earn successful outcomes in that environment. They know how that situation affected their hype level and their performance. They know what the excitement felt like, and they realize that in these situations, champions use the extra adrenaline to enhance their performance without losing their self-control. They do not play worse ("choke") or the same: they play better. Their superb physical and mental skills actually allow them to use the excitement of the situation to lift up their game to new heights.

An athlete may not have played for a championship at the level she is now competing at, but she has been in exciting situations before. She should use the experiences she already has to build up her confidence and prepare effectively. She must find a way to control her hype level and create her ideal performance state. Whether she is too low or too high, she can invoke the strategies listed above and "act as if" her hype level is just right.

Acting Class

> It's natural to feel anxiety, but you hide it. Show it and you are through.
> —Joe Garagiola, Baseball Player and Sportscaster

> Just because you are worried doesn't mean you have to act worried. Always behave confidently.
> —Dr. Rob Gilbert, Sport Psychologist

> You ought to run the hardest when you feel the worst. Never let the other guy know you're down.
> —Joe DiMaggio, Baseball Hall of Famer

If an athlete is feeling down, she should think of how she would prefer to feel and act that way. If she is dragging, she should act enthusiastic. If she is scared, she should act courageous. If she feels defeated, she should act confident. If she is hurt, she should act invincible. Junior Seau was a tragic master of this. He refused to show any weaknesses and his ability to act invincible led to success on the field. Anything done without any counter-balance is likely to have a long-term negative consequence, but his on-field success included 12 Pro-Bowl selections and a spot on the NFL 1990's All-Decade team. In the 1994 AFC Championship game versus Pittsburgh, Seau played with a pinched nerve in his neck and recorded 16 tackles. His Chargers won 17-13. Seau committed suicide in 2012.

Two reasons exist to act as if you already are how you want to be. First, communication. The majority of communications is non-verbal. There is a loop between attitudes and body language: each affects the other. Acting tough makes it is easier to think tough thoughts. Communication to teammates and opponents is also important. An athlete should not let others know about her problems on the field (private discussions are a different matter). Opponents who recognize her absence of poise, confidence, or enthusiasm are themselves infused with confidence. On the other hand, teammates get pulled down with her. Teams often flow into a great run together, but they can just as easily "slump" together if they lack the mental toughness to know their jobs and do their jobs. Attitudes are contagious and leaders embrace this fact, knowing that they can lead with confidence and positive energy even if their outcomes are not good today.

Second, acting as if will often help a person to become what they wanted to become. The act stops being an act and becomes the new reality quicker than expected. Charlie Brown said in an old cartoon that "if you're going to get any joy out of being depressed, the worst thing you can do is straighten up and hold your head high because then you'll start to feel better." Pretending to be confident, enthusiastic, or pain-free often leads to that reality. (The opposite is also true, as demonstrated by hypochondriacs.) The "act" is a self-fulfilling prophecy.

How does a leader act as if she already is what she is trying to become? Attitude and body language. "If you would be powerful, pretend to be powerful," goes the old saying. An athlete can take a deep breath, pull her sternum up, and use an optimistic explanatory style of self-talk to create her ideal performance state for the task at hand. She imagines what it would be like to feel the way she desires and imitates the physiology that she had when she felt that way in the past[12]; or she mimics how other people look when they behave that way. The physiology to mimic includes posture, breathing patterns, facial expressions, movements, and tonality of both thoughts and spoken words.

Figure 10-4

An athlete may be "scared to death" to step into a situation such as facing an intimidating opponent or playing in front of a large audience, but that fear does not have to hurt her performance. She should ask herself, "How would I act if I were totally confident right now?" and then act that way. It is not as difficult as it may sound; she can be totally confident that she will give her best effort now. Being scared is not a bad thing; only acting scared is.

> **"Acting as if" is better than "fake it 'til you make it" because it is impossible to lie to yourself.**

---

[12] From her P.P.P.P. (personal past peak performance).

Body Language Speaks

> Do not let what you cannot do interfere with what you can do.
> —John Wooden

> I am careful not to give in to theatrics when times are tough.
> —Tony LaRussa, Baseball Manager

> Emotions make excellent servants, but tyrannical masters.
> —John Seymour, Author and Activist

Poise is the outward demonstration of self-control. Self-control starts with controlling hype level and continues with effective self-talk and attitudes. Having poise is a great idea because it usually indicates internal control. Control is the critical issue (not just keeping the coach happy). During a performance, self-control helps the athlete appear confident to herself, her teammates, her opponents, and her audience.

If an athlete maintains her self-control, she will always have poise, but she could fake poise without having self-control. Many athletes appear poised, but are in complete turmoil on the inside. This typically happens because the athlete has learned to follow team rules about throwing helmets and gloves. She has been taught to maintain poise at all times, but does not understand how self-control impacts performance. She is not "acting as if" she is under control, she is just faking it. Faking it may help a little, but her thoughts are not faking anything. On the inside, she is a mess so the body language/self-talk loop is fractured. Externally, she may not display much negative body language. Unfortunately, if she lacks control on the inside, her performance will still suffer. Athletes who fail to recognize the importance of self-control will not make appropriate adjustments, thus setting the stage for a poor performance. Their poor responses to adversity lead to poor approaches on the next play. Mental skills training empowers athletes to maintain control on the inside, making the outward demonstration of poise second nature.

Figure 10-5: Within Wooden's Pyramid of Success

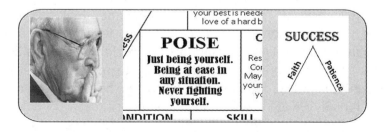

Tight as a Drum, Loose as a Goose

> Hitting balls off the tee is monotonous, but it's important, too. Repetition breeds familiarity. Familiarity breeds comfort. Comfort breeds relaxation and the best environment for achieving success is when you're relaxed.
> —Derek Jeter, Baseball Player

> The main thing is to try to relax, to stay loose. If I try to muscle the ball, I'll be off.
> —George Blanda, Football Hall of Fame Quarterback / Kicker

> God, grant me the strength to swing easier.
> —A golfer's prayer

Tension is literally the contraction of muscle fibers. Relaxation is simply the release of this tension. The goal is to maximize explosiveness by relaxing, which is to say by contracting particular muscle groups not-at-all. Only two steps are required for relaxation: awareness and release. Unfortunately, both steps can be difficult.

Learning to relax is critical for performance for several reasons. First, relaxed muscles fire with greater power than tense ones. Second, a tensed muscle is more susceptible to injury than a relaxed one. Third, tense muscles use energy that would be more useful elsewhere. Fourth, they impede the movement of other muscles. Having an appropriate muscle firing pattern (great rhythm) means that the muscles needed to perform effectively can work hard (use energy) while other muscles stay relaxed (do not use energy). How can a smaller girl have more power than a bigger girl? The answer lies in each athlete's functional strength and her mechanics. Her mechanics are defined by the order and efficiency of her muscle contractions; her efficiency increases when she starts from a relaxed state.

Between awareness and release of tension, awareness is typically the tougher skill to master. An athlete does not know what she does not know. Tension builds but remains unidentified, thus hindering performance. To release tension consciously rather than wait for it to go away by chance, awareness is required.

Some people have performed some tasks so many times with excess tension that they can execute surprisingly well. An athlete should not think that tension cannot be released or that relaxation will not make the performance even better. With improvements in self-control and relaxation, good performances can become great. Like all skills, hype level control and the ability to relax take time to develop. Also, like other skills, relaxation and self-control can be learned by anyone: strive for perfection, though it would be a mistake to expect it.

Numerous relaxation strategies exist; they can be categorized into immediate strategies designed to release undesired tension right now, and long-term strategies that can prevent the tension from ever happening. Relaxation is simply zero contraction and the simplest answer for getting rid of tension immediately is often the most effective: just let it go. Simply exhaling and releasing identified tension often works. If not, stretching and focusing on that muscle group may help. A contrast strategy whereby the muscle is contracted as tightly as possible and held for a few seconds and then released is another possibility. So is massage.

Figure 10-6

Progressive relaxation is a systematic contrast strategy that works from the toes all the way up the body. The athlete lies on her back and regulates her breathing, meaning that she focuses solely on her breath, slowing it down and deepening each breath. She relaxes by tightening muscle groups as much as possible for a few seconds, then relaxing them during exhalation. She progresses up from the toes to the forehead. For example, she would tighten and release the toes and feet first and then the calves, the quadriceps, the hamstrings, and so on up the body. This technique promotes focus and relaxation, and it can also be used to promote sleep.[13]

Long-term fixes for tension include improved posture, increased confidence, a healthy perspective, empathy, forgiveness, improved communication, and a positive attitude. Posture is challenging to improve because it often requires thought about something that normally occurs without thought. In addition to improving posture simply with will power, yoga, Pilates, aerobic exercise, and other exercise regimens can have dramatic positive effects. So can Rolfing, a

---

[13] A mental training, progressive relaxation, and guided imagery compact disc specifically for the softball pitcher or softball hitter is available from the author at www.CoachTraub.com.

sophisticated and typically painful series of deep-tissue massages. These strategies challenge the body and mind simultaneously.

Comfort leads to relaxation, and familiarity breeds comfort. Unfamiliar situations that can cause tension include playing in a new place (a road game), playing in front of a person perceived to be particularly important, and playing against an exceptional opponent. To be comfortable in an unfamiliar situation, leaders emphasize familiar elements, just as Coach Dale did in *Hoosiers* when he measured the height of the basket in the huge arena for his small-town Hickory High School Huskers before the state championship game. Familiar elements to emphasize include the athlete's routine and her constant goal of doing her best by controlling the controllables.

Much of mental skills training is ultimately aimed at helping athletes find their trust mode so they can relax and play the game. Imagery allows athletes to get the "feel" of a situation before it happens. Confidence also affects comfort. Learning to consciously increase confidence helps athletes relax, as does maintaining a positive attitude and a mature perspective. Refrain: leaders are mentally tough because they relax and habitually do what it takes to give their best effort.

Breathe or Die

I look at victory as milestones on a very long highway.
—Joan Benoit Samuelson, Olympic Marathon Gold Medalist

The most commonly used strategy for gathering self-control and relaxation, for good reason, is to breathe deeply. Leaders typically incorporate a deep breath or two into their routines. Without ever practicing deep breathing, most athletes fail to receive all its benefits. It is a common mistake to take a big breath that is not as deep in the lungs as it could be. This is still useful, just not as valuable as it could be. To practice, inhale through the nose as much air as is comfortably possible. Go deep by filling the lungs from bottom to top by thirds (think "bottom - near the stomach," "middle – expand the ribs," and "top – lift the chest"). Exhale in a slow and steady manner from the top of the lungs down, reversing the process. Finish by contracting the abdomen muscles to squeeze more air out of the bottom of the lungs. Try to smooth out the connection between inhalation and exhalation. To help this connection and promote full use of the lungs, occasionally tap on the top of the head with the middle three fingertips in the middle towards the front. (This final piece of advice may seem strange to most people, as it originally did to the author, but it seems to help. Test it out. Take a deep breath without tapping, then add the tapping to see if a bit more air enters the lungs!)

Relax during the exhalation. Use it to cue the release of unwanted tension, pulling the sternum up and the shoulders down and back. Depending on the situation and the person, the exhale can be through the mouth making a "hhhhhh" sound or through the nose. It can be fairly quick, but one popular practice is to give it twice as much time as the inhalation. If it is not smooth and steady, hype level is too high and gathering is needed to regain self-control. Use the amount of "choppiness" in the exhalation as an indication for how much time should be allowed for gathering.

Figure 10-7

EXERCISE

Sit up or stand up and practice taking five deep breaths right now, filling the lungs as fully as is comfortable. Inhale through your nose, filling your lungs from the bottom first. Fill up the lungs by bringing air to the stomach, expanding ribs, then lift the chest. Exhale slowly and steadily from the top of the lungs down. Try to connect each breath to the next one. Count to four on the inhalation and eight on the exhalation.

Don't Just Win, Be Two Better

A winner will find a way to win. Winners take bad breaks and use them to drive themselves to be that much better. Quitters take bad breaks and use them as a reason to give up. It's all a matter of pride.
—Nancy Lopez, Hall-of-Fame Golfer

In competition, even mature athletes can lose their ideal performance state when something outside of their control frustrates them. For example, a pitcher may throw a great pitch, only to have the batter hit an off-balance blooper in front of the outfielders. The pitcher could have appropriate self-talk, saying that she is doing her job well and life and softball are not fair. However, upon recognizing the importance of that play on the scoreboard, this athlete or her teammates may lose the feelings of enthusiasm and confidence that were previously allowing a loose and relaxed performance. Her frustration at real events outside her control has thrown her off kilter. She has lost her "green light" state. A team that is thrown off balance in this way may appear to implode or "choke."

A good attitude to promote an ideal state through any adversity comes from the thought, "Be two better." The idea is to enter every contest with a resolution to be significantly better than the opponent: not two strikes, two plays, or two runs -- just two somethings. Two represents a concept that is more than one. Therefore, no single occurrence of misfortune can cause a "failure" to meet this goal. Neither will one great play ever satisfy this goal. This goal helps leaders stay on an even keel. If an athlete's goal is to win the contest (which is not recommended, but it will still occur), bad luck could cause her to "fail" despite being "one" better. If she is "two better," she is sure to win.

Figure 10-8

CHAPTER 11

ACHIEVEMENTS IN SOFTBALL ARE FUN... AND SO ARE SETBACKS

I kind of forced myself to say, 'Hey, I'm going to enjoy this moment,
it may not happen again.'
—Michael Jordan, Basketball Hall of Famer

When you take a person and put him in a situation where he is having fun,
his possibilities are limitless.
—Marshall Faulk, Football Hall of Famer

I've learned if you have the chance, you'd better take it. Life's too precious.
I always tell my players to "Enjoy the now."
—Gary Williams, Basketball Coach

You go for it. All the stops are out. Caution is to the wind, and you're battling with
everything you have. That's the real fun of the game.
—Dan Dierdorf, Football Player and Announcer

I tell myself just to go out and play the game as I did when I was a kid.
—Tom Watson, Golfer

I know a lot of people think the training is monotonous, but it's not if you're enjoying
what you're doing. I love to swim and I love to train.
—Tracy Caulkins, Olympic Swimmer

We play with enthusiasm and recklessness. We aren't afraid to lose. If we win, great.
But win or lose, it is the competition that gives us pleasure.
—Joe Paterno, Football Coach

In a discussion of attitude for optimal performance, it would be difficult to overstate the importance of having fun. Having fun is a foreign concept to no one, yet athletes often forget to do it. Many reasons exist for this forgetfulness, and a psychological study of every personality type is beyond the scope of this book. What is not beyond its scope is encouragement for each athlete to study herself, develop her awareness, and then coach herself to have fun playing the game. This may be the most important point inside these pages.

Fun happens when the athlete is in the moment. Leaders do not arrive at fun. An athlete is either having fun or she is not having fun. Letting go of concern for outcomes allows enjoyment to happen. More fun leads to better performances and the positive snowball effect is rolling!

Enjoyment, practice, success, pain, "failure," winning, losing, progress, and achievement are all part of the athlete's process of finding out how good she can be. The process can simultaneously be tiring and fun, exciting and fun, nerve-wracking and fun, even painful and fun. It would be difficult, however, to have fun while being frustrated, impatient, lethargic, annoyed, angry, stubborn, or resentful. Sports should be fun, so athletes must work on their skill at avoiding these negative emotions. If they find this difficult, the current goal is to avoid them more, perhaps by 10%. Motif: strive for perfection, but never expect it.

Fun is a "green light" indicator. Absence of it indicates a "yellow light" or "red light." Some athletes notice a little smile just before performing. Others have a bounce in their step, their sternum up, shoulders back, and their head held high. Perhaps one athlete's enthusiasm creates a noticeable feeling in her stomach that says, "Let's go!" The looseness and absence of worry that accompany this attitude enable her to give her best effort. A lack of it causes problems. Sometimes, an athlete who believes she is slumping looks to change all sorts of physical mechanics when all she really needs to do is change her attitude and start having fun again.

Figure 11-1

Consistently giving best effort performances is difficult. Difficult and fun do not typically go together, but they do in softball. It is good that it is difficult because for one team to win, the other has to lose. As the proverb goes, "if you want to get things that others won't get, you have to do things that others won't do." Most teams do not consistently practice at the edge of their ability levels both physically and mentally. They do not embrace challenges and stay positive through adversity. Most teams will sweat and bleed, but most do not know how to 'win' the mental side of the game every day.

Practice should be fun. Baseball Coach Augie Garrido says, "Enjoy building the ingredients of success." Short periods may occur in which it is not loads of fun, but leaders usually have a good attitude while working at their craft. Some drills will certainly be more fun than others, but if every athlete reminds herself why she does them, she can learn to enjoy them all. Frequent reminders to maintain an enthusiastic attitude and very short-term goals may be needed when the going gets tough. For some, learning to love challenges and struggles takes time. Then, when the most challenging, "clutch" situations occur, the athlete can enjoy the opportunities it brings and perform up to her potential.

Figure 11-2

Any optional endeavor that requires a great amount of time and energy should be fun most of the time. If softball is usually fun, then the overall pursuit is worthwhile. However, if an athlete seldom derives any enjoyment from practice, she should reevaluate her reasons for playing. She will often find that she has forgotten why she loves the game. She may find that she is playing for someone other than herself. Leaders quickly answer the question, "Who is the most important person for you to please with your performance?" Hesitation is a warning signal that the athlete is not choosing to compete. If she cannot choose to compete, perhaps a different pursuit would make better use of her time. It would be a poor idea, of course, to make major life decisions hastily, and it would certainly be inappropriate to panic over a single bad day or week. Ultimately, though, an athlete should be able to say that she enjoys her sport inherently.

A softball player who shows up to practice, physically, but would rather be elsewhere will not get better, faster. She may need to take a break. She may have to spend some time evaluating her values and priorities. If she finally concludes that she is choosing to compete, great. Now, she must find a way to make her pursuit of approaching her potential more fun. Perhaps a different practice partner would help her regain the attitude she seeks. Sometimes rearrangement of drills or scheduling can help an athlete out of a funk. It is a good idea to end workouts with a task that is particularly enjoyable so that the players will be more likely to have a good attitude about softball until their next practice. Having fun is important; if what the athletes are doing is not working, change something.

Quite a few athletes only have fun when they get positive outcomes. This perspective is not healthy. Of course, it is more fun to do well than to do poorly, and it is fine for enjoyment to increase when outcomes are superb. However, the game should be inherently fun. "I love making a diving catch," or "I love hitting a round ball with a round bat, squarely," is much better than "I love softball." Inherent enjoyment of the game allows the athlete to create the fun attitude before she has any positive outcomes to lean on that day. The athlete who needs to play well to have any confidence and enjoyment is doomed to inconsistency.

Finally, when an athlete comes to the end (of the game, season, or her career), she should enjoy the last performance most. It is what she has prepared for. Her preparation included almost immeasurable hard work. It also included the pain of setbacks, the challenges of adjustments, and the satisfaction of achievements. It would make no sense not to enjoy the culmination of such an effort. Some people may perceive enormous pressure and forget the joys that this moment holds, but leaders will not. Whatever outcomes lie ahead, this performance will define how good she can be at this point in her life. If she has no regrets about her preparation, then she has already succeeded. Hopefully, this peace of mind and her natural ability will be enough to provide the outcome that she has dreamed of. Win or lose, though, she is a winner in the eyes of mature observers, herself the most important among them. The entire process of approaching her potential has been fun, but no experience could be more fun than this culminating moment. When they arrive at the mountaintop, leaders enjoy the view!

PART 3:

GET READY, GET SET

*Always bear in mind that your own resolution to succeed is
more important than any other thing.*
—Abraham Lincoln

An athlete's approach begins the performance cycle: approach, perform, and respond. Her response leads directly to her next approach. Attitude impacts every step of the way. This section evaluates the components of an effective approach. It attempts to explain specifically how to set the stage for a peak performance on one play. Doing so will both maximize her chances for being in the zone and enable her to perform the best she can at that moment in time, even if she is not experiencing a peak performance. All of an athlete's preparations put together will be long, challenging, and tough. And fun.

An athlete's approach includes imaging success (Chapter 12) and preparing at practice (Chapter 13). There are no shortcuts to success, especially since success is defined by effort. Chapters 14 through 16 deal with the part of an approach that occurs immediately before a performance. At this point, practice is over. Finding the most effective approach, however, is far from complete. It is time to use the mind to get ready to produce outstanding results (and partially uncontrollable outcomes).

Leaders know how to work smart. They do not think that showing up, doing what they are told, and hustling makes them a coach's dream. They recognize that all of that is important, but to be a coach's dream, they have to do more. They coach themselves to get better, faster, by having high standards and paying attention to details. They find ways to work just beyond the top edge of their current ability level, despite the pain involved. In fact, they learn to get used to and even welcome this pain, recognizing it as a positive sign of their progress. They use imagery, paying attention to when and how it has the biggest positive impact. They constantly ask questions during practice and push themselves to work on their weaknesses.

To put it simply, leaders do more than what is expected and more than others are likely to do. They study the intricacies of the game even when they are not at practice. They pursue strategic plans that truly maximize their chances for great outcomes, including carefully designing and executing pre-game, pre-performance, and gathering routines. They are eager to test any mental skills tools that can aid their consistency such as cues, power phrases, imagery, and even anchors.

Chapter 12

Begin with the End in Mind (Imagery)

The moment of enlightenment is when a person's dreams of possibilities
become images of probabilities.
—Vic Braden, Tennis Instructor

I close my eyes and see the shot. I look at the ball and see the type of shot I have
in my mind. I see it fly and I see it land. It's a way of seeing the result
before you do it. I visualize the end result.
—Annika Sorenstam, Golfer

Imagery is using the mind to create or recreate an experience using as many senses as possible. The human brain does not differentiate between a real experience and a vividly imagined one. Therefore, experience can make an athlete better and imagery can, too... in exactly the same way. The great thing about imagery is that it is free, always available, and (with practice) completely controllable.

One consistent characteristic of leaders in athletics is that they are consumed with excellence. They think about winning and how to win more than average performers. Usually a lot more. They may even go overboard in the sport/lifestyle balance issue because they are so consumed with their sport. They imagine greatness in their sport so often that they arrive at both practices and performances with clear goals. Plus, they have already seen themselves achieving these goals in their heads. They begin with the end already clearly in mind.

Imagery can be used in many specific ways. It can be used to learn a new skill, to rehearse a skill or pre-performance routine, or to create an ideal state. Before a big game, an athlete may imagine her personal past peak performance (P.P.P.P.) to increase her confidence or a day at the beach to help her relax and slow the game down. Imagery can be used during a game to program the body and mind, like when a pitcher images the precise trajectory of her pitch. It can be used after the contest to help make appropriate adjustments. Imaging what happened helps athletes recall what went right and what went wrong. Then, imaging what they would like to happen the next time that situation occurs links their positive response to a good next approach. Both scientific research and experiential evidence indicate that using imagery enhances performance. As with any skill, improvement at imagery comes from quality practice.

Figure 12-1

Most thinking is done with words. Imagery is not done with words; it is practiced by imagining a scenario with any or all of the senses. Since a majority of information is taken in through the eyes, much of the power of imagery comes via visualization. Adding other senses strengthens imagery's impact. One at a time, an athlete can add in how it smells, feels, tastes, and/or sounds. Typically, emphasis for an athlete is on how it feels and looks.

Everyone can benefit from imagery and everyone daydreams, which is a basic form of imagery. Quality practice is the key to maximizing the benefit of this free, universally available training tool. A primary goal of imagery is to *feel* the experience happening, rather than merely thinking about it. With practice, component skills such as number of senses used, vividness, controllability, and self-awareness will improve. So, too, will the ability to stay with the imagined experience longer.

It is difficult to prove exactly why imagery works, although the evidence is incontrovertible. Academic studies have consistently shown a positive, measurable effect. Analysis of data from various research studies has shown that well over 90 percent of Olympians use imagery for competition preparation. Plenty of anecdotal evidence also exists. In one study, a coach/researcher helped one group of Olympic hopeful downhill skiers practice imagery before each run but did not help

a control group. The control group skiers could use imagery on their own if they wanted, but they were not given any guidance. The positive effect was so strong that the coach/researcher abandoned the experiment halfway through because he no longer wanted to deprive the control group of the imagery training.
Images should be positive. Recalling peak performances and personal triumphs does wonders for an athlete's confidence. Imaging future good behavior programs the body and mind, increasing the chance of executing that skill. Imaging negative experiences can have the expected effect of degrading a performance, although this does not mean that athletes should only image perfect performances. A huge part of being an effective athlete is being able to effectively deal with adversity. Therefore, leaders also image their desired behaviors following a mistake or bad luck[14].

It can be beneficial for an athlete to image significant past personal experiences. Both positive and negative experiences can help bring strong emotions and intense energy from the past to the present. She may have to spend some time searching her personal database of memories to dig up the experiences that will help her the most. She should look for the events that motivate and generate energy. If she chooses to recall a negative experience, she should remind herself of how she overcame or was able to move beyond this adversity. She will gain energy and determination from the negative image while still leaving the practice on a positive note.

Most professional and Olympic athletes use imagery systematically to enhance their performance. Learning imagery can initially be intimidating, but it should not be. It simply takes quality practice and experimentation! Of course, a beginner is not particularly skilled at imagery, but this is good news because there is plenty of room to learn and receive imagery's benefits! It is a good idea to designate a specific spot exclusively for practicing imagery and other mental skills. It does not have to be fancy, just secluded. For example, facing the opposite direction in bed might be a place that works. This designated mental practice spot should be normally available, private, quiet, and comfortable.

Consistent practice will pay off. First, practice simple scenes in real time. Control an image much like operating a remote control, trying not to use the fast forward button too much. Images can be in the first person, meaning that the athlete sees the scene as she will see it in real life, or in third person, meaning that it appears as if it is on a movie screen. When using third-person imagery, the perspective can be from in front, behind, above, or anywhere else. The image can be small, medium, or panoramic; color or black and white. No wrong way to practice exists, though

---

[14] See the Doomsday Flashcard Exercise in this chapter.

first-person imagery is by far the most popular method practiced by experienced athletes. Once the athlete sees the scene clearly, she should remember to add in the other senses: how does this field smell, the crowd sound, and the impact feel?

Imagery can be incorporated into an athlete's routine plan for each play. Immediately before each play, a quick image or two of what should or could happen next allows the body to be truly prepared to act or react aggressively, under control. This commits the body to a specific plan, allowing instincts to take over during the action. For example, an outfielder may see herself making a great catch to rob a home run. Next, she could imagine herself cutting off a single in the gap and making a great throw to second base. Then, she might include one of two reactions to a looping liner in front of her that she may be able to catch. If she is in a "no doubles" defense, she would imagine slowing down to keep the ball in front of her. If an out is more valued than keeping the batter to a single, she would see herself making a great diving catch.

EXERCISE

Imagery Practice

Take a few moments now to experience the power of imagery. Take a deep belly breath and relax. Imagine that you are holding your hand out and a good friend gives you three lemon drop candies. Watch as your friend drops them into your palm one at a time. Think about their shape, color, and feel in your hand. Pause your reading to do this now.

Next, anticipate putting the candies into your mouth. Briefly pause your reading here. Now, imagine putting all three lemon drops in your mouth. Leave one in the middle of your mouth and move one to each cheek. Suck the sour and sweet juice out of the candies. Pause your reading here to enjoy the tasty sensation.

Did your salivary glands activate? If so, you have experienced a real physiological effect from a totally imagined experience. If not, you were not as absorbed into the imagery practice as you could be. Try it again when you can avoid distractions to practice increasing the power of imagery.

Imagery helps the mind and body cooperate with each other. Without it, an athlete may hear instructions to do something and even tell herself to do it. Then, she may do the exact opposite of what she just agreed to do. For example, the first base coach may say "freeze on a line drive." The runner may nod in agreement, and then make the mistake of running a couple steps toward the next base when that line drive is hit. It is not that the runner is purposefully ignoring the instruction, but rather that she never fully committed her mind to that plan. Imagery ensures this commitment and adds a bonus of a mental rehearsal of the play, too.

Incorporating imagery into a routine of preparation and/or reflection is an excellent way to practice it. Typically, imaging appropriate attitudes, postures, and behaviors before performing helps enable that "green light" "Go, go, go!" feeling. Various external images can be tried. The image of a glass lake helps many to quiet their conscious mind. The image of Supergirl, Rocky, or their favorite player helps many to feel powerful. The brief image of a strong, shiny, silver spring all coiled up and waiting to pounce can be a powerful image for athletes like hitters who use quick, explosive movements. The calmness and beauty of the image just before a perfectly synchronized explosion of resources helps the athlete to stay patient, then explode. Often, players image an entire performance before it happens so that they will feel like they have been there before when it actually happens. This is a bit like taking a Mulligan in golf... without cheating.

After performing, imagery can promote effective adjustments. Pausing during an inning to mull over what just happened, especially if it was a mistake, is usually not a good idea. During the game, athletes want to stay in the present by releasing mistakes and trusting their ability. Later, imaging what happened can aid their powers of recall, helping them to not miss the opportunity to learn and grow. A leader picks out which behaviors to repeat and which to change, and then images herself executing the corrections.

An athlete's performance, in imagery as in sport, is her responsibility. To approach her potential, she will have to figure out how to maximize imagery's benefits. No single formula works for everyone. With motivation and the courage to try new strategies, she will develop her skill and awareness, practicing what works and enjoying the effects of tapping into the power of her mind.

EXERCISE

Doomsday Flashcards

Prepare flashcards of your top 10-15 most stressful forms of adversity that may come up during a game by recording each scenario on a notecard. Pick a card, and then image dealing effectively with that challenge! This will force you to formulate a plan and provide a mental rehearsal for executing it. Leaders use this to avoid the negative snowball effect. Such an effect gains momentum when the adversity is a surprise. Remember to quickly go to forgiveness if the negative emotion is stuck in consciousness. You should feel yourself getting the "monkey" off your back, refocusing on the task at hand, and concluding this process by imaging an effective performance on the next play.

EXERCISE

Directive Affirmations

Imagery is a superb tool for tapping into the immense power of the subconscious mind. One method is to take a few minutes shortly after waking each morning to image the successful completion of today's greatest challenges. This may seem like it is too simple to be effective, but try it for a week and see if you are not impressed by the results.

Another powerful strategy is to write a paragraph about an important goal and place it in five places that you see often. Examples places include the refrigerator door, the bathroom mirror, the car's dashboard, on the kitchen table, and on your cell phone. Every time you see this paragraph, read it again and either image one of the steps for achieving the goal or imagine how great it will be to reach the goal.

To write the paragraph, start with a description of the goal stated in the first-person, present tense. ("I am the starting pitcher for my team.") Next, remind yourself of why this is such an important goal. Follow that with the specifics about how this goal will be reached. Add one final sentence: the first sentence precisely repeated. Run this 'program' for 21 days, remembering to both read and practice imagery each time.

CHAPTER 13

I WILL NOT BE DENIED (PREPARATION)

You do not find out who "wants it more" on game day. You find out on all the other days.

Confidence doesn't come out of nowhere. It's a result of something... hours and days and weeks and years of constant work and dedication.
—Roger Staubach, Football Hall of Famer

Luck is what happens when preparation meets opportunity.
—Carlos Tosca, Baseball Manager

There's no such thing as natural touch. Touch is something you create by hitting millions of golf balls.
—Lee Trevino, Golfer

You can't make a great play unless you do it first in practice.
—Chuck Noll, Football Coach

Preparation is a necessity for approaching potential. Great things do not happen without effort. Even those athletes with wonderful genetic gifts must prepare well to perform well when the level of competition gets high enough. The controllable goal of approaching potential is not dependent on the athlete's genetics but on her industriousness (Coach Wooden's word for working hard and smart).

A leader prepares effectively by having a passion for the game, a love of competition, and a disciplined work ethic. Wanting to win as much as possible requires a great effort, including placing what she needs in front of what she wants. She puts growth before comfort and truth before ego. Often, a champion will work when others are resting. Sometimes, she needs physical rest when she would rather continue training. In preparation, as in all things, attitude significantly impacts the quality of the work being done. A leader enjoys the "grind" of training. She knows that she is working hard to achieve her goals, and this self-esteem boost makes it possible for her to stay confident and positive through challenging circumstances.

Great athletes will not be denied. They simply want to win more than mediocre athletes. This is not apparent because they try harder during the performance. Most players are highly motivated during the game. Competitiveness is revealed during practice and away from the diamond. Leaders get better, faster, because they are consumed with thoughts about what it takes to be successful. When others are "taking a break," they are wondering what is possible, dreaming up new experiments, vividly imagining wild successes, and storing up excitement for the next time they get to compete with themselves in practice or in a game.

Leaders do "it" right. "It" means everything, which is a million times easier to say than do because everything includes big tiring jobs and tedious items that may seem almost trivial. For example, when practicing a 60-foot sprint, a leader sprints at least 60 yards, not 57. When in doubt, she does an extra to ensure doing it right. She practices with a specific purpose, rather than just to get repetitions. For example, she aims each throw for a small target rather than just a general area, such as her teammate. She takes practice repetitions at game speed rather than at a comfortable speed... until these two become identical. In everything she does, a right way and a "not right" way exist. The "not right" way is not necessarily wrong, but observant athletes know that it is not the best way—it is not the right way.

Leaders want to be the best they can be, and they know this means consistent attention to details. This attention allows them to know, rather than guess, that they are doing things right. No one is perfect, and it would be flat out wrong to expect perfection. It would also be wrong not to strive for perfection. Leaders are honest with themselves and others by accepting responsibility, avoiding excuses, and doing their best to do things right, one step at a time.

A solid physical foundation through hard work in practice prepares an athlete for positive outcomes. This foundation includes weight training and conditioning, as well as practicing her position's specific mechanics. She should understand the importance and the place of her physical mechanics: namely, achieving muscle memory for doing things right. Proper mechanics give her the highest probability of a positive outcome. By teaching her body what to do in practice, execution becomes automatic before it is time to perform. During a performance, therefore, she does not have to think about *how* to do it right. In fact, reflections of confidence should be the only thoughts she has about her physical foundation during performances, allowing her focus during play to be free to go to the proper external cues[15].

Once an athlete has the best muscle memory she can acquire at this point in her life, she still has more preparation to do. Most players at this point feel like they have already given enough of themselves; a leader can and is eager to handle more. She prepares herself to give her best effort by taking care of her body. Nutrition, rest, and care for her body in and out of the training room are critical, though their details are beyond the scope of this book. She also must prepare her mental game by having balance, a healthy perspective, and an effective pre-performance routine to get mentally and physically ready to perform.

Little is Big, Big is Little (Attention to Details)

Seemingly trivial matters, taken together and added to many, many other so-called trivial matters, build into something very big: namely, your success.
—John Wooden

There is no such thing as a small flaw.
—Don Shula, Football Coach

John Wooden was the head coach of seven consecutive national championship teams at UCLA. He emphasized the importance of attention to details to the players he coached. Wooden wrote the following:

> *I believe in the basics: attention to, and perfection of, tiny details that might commonly be overlooked. They may seem trivial, perhaps even laughable to those who don't understand, but they aren't. They are fundamental to your progress in basketball, business, and life. They are the difference between champions and near champions. For example, at the first squad meeting each season, held two weeks before our first actual practice, I personally demonstrated how I wanted players to put on their socks each and every time.*

Why did Wooden personally show his players how he wanted them to put on socks? This demonstration conveyed two important points. First, the direct point is that wrinkles, folds, and creases can cause blisters, so this attention to detail is a way for each player to take responsibility for his own health. The second point is that attention to many "little" details was critical to the success of the UCLA

---

[15] Chapter 18 discusses this detail of a proper focus.

Bruins. They were leaders dedicated to excellence; they did common things in uncommon ways. Despite the players' initial reaction of surprise and usually a little laughter, this sage advice was what they were looking for from their famous coach.

Normal athletes think, though not too much, about little things. Leaders call them "little things" and think about them often. What is a "little thing?" Perhaps finding a tip-off that indicates the pitcher is throwing a change-up an instant before she releases it? Perhaps knowing when it is better to slide feet first or head first? Perhaps an infielder's footwork on a slow rolling backhand play is a "little thing?" The answers could be the difference between early or on time, safe or out, accurate throw or error, score or out, and injured or healthy. Are any of these "little things?"

Doing things right will make the difference, in the long run, between winning and losing. In the short run, the difference may be hard to notice, but the details define the difference between good and best effort. Every "little" thing is actually a "big thing" because the slightest edge just might make the difference on any one play, and any one play can easily make the difference between winning and losing (either directly or by its impact on momentum).

Figure 13-1

Leaders discipline themselves to do all the big things (what others call little things) correctly over and over again. Practice makes permanent. Therefore, every task or drill performed in practice provides an opportunity to rehearse mental discipline. People are creatures of habit, so a leader works hard and smart not only to improve her skill, but also to build quality habits. In games, her mental discipline will be reflected in her relentless approach to each play. In practice, awareness of details and having a purpose for every action allows her to do things right. She will develop correct muscle memory, allowing her to perform her mechanics correctly in "pressure-filled" situations without thinking about them (provided her hype number is under control). Her overall mental discipline will improve, meaning that her focus and concentration skills improve, too. Also, the depth of her knowledge about herself and her sport will increase faster than if she coasts during practice. Finally, she will be a positive influence on her teammates.

Although the concepts involved in being mentally strong are not complicated, they are certainly challenging. Great athletes find a way to give their best effort one step at a time, in large part by paying attention to the details.

Becoming "Clutch"

> You can't practice one way and then expect to do it differently in a game.
> —Al Kaline, Baseball Hall of Famer

> It's not necessarily the amount of time you spend at practice that counts;
> it's what you put into the practice.
> —Eric Lindros, Hockey Player

> Concentration is why some athletes are better than others.... You develop that concentration in training. You can't be lackadaisical in training and concentrate in a meet.
> —Edwin Moses, Olympic Gold Medalist, he won 122 straight hurdle races over 11 years

The goal of coming as close as possible to reaching potential is both noble and daunting. While an athlete's knowledge and skill will improve over her career, one aspect of approaching potential is that when it is time to perform, she is consistently near the peak of her current skill level in tough situations. Preparation is the primary ingredient for performing well in the "clutch." Quality of practice affects every aspect of skill, including muscle memory, confidence, and awareness.

Hype level is often dissimilar from practices to games. Athletes are typically too low at practice and too high "when it counts."[16] Therefore, the goal is typically to raise hype level in practice and lower it in games. Several strategies for lowering arousal levels in competition were presented in Chapter 10, including maintaining a healthy perspective, thinking effectively, breathing deeply, and using imagery and routines.

---

[16] (The critical point here is that it always counts! *Now + now + now = life!*)

This discussion focuses on raising the intensity level, or caring more, at practice. The concept that game days are more important than other days is a flawed one. Coach Wooden's father taught him to make each day his masterpiece and the father of NFL Head Coaches John and Jim Harbaugh (the opposing head coaches in the 2013 Super Bowl) taught them to "attack this day with enthusiasm unknown to mankind." Today is all an athlete can control, and it is when approaching potential happens. Winning begins now!

A leader cares about her performance in practice as much (or almost as much) as her performance in competition. American society leads the other way. Practice outcomes do not have as many ramifications as game outcomes. The prevailing attitude is that it is okay to take a "do-over" in practice, even though no do-overs exist in competition. Certainly more practice is appropriate when mistakes are being made, but the next one can never *make up* for a mistake on the last one. Life provides no opportunities for do-overs.

To get closer to the goal of having a similar hype number in practices and games, athletes need to understand how they could *theoretically* care about a practice repetition as much as a similar post-season repetition with the entire team's playoff life hanging in the balance. This begins by having the primary goal of approaching potential... being the best athlete she can be. Achieving this gives her peace of mind *and* maximizes her chances to get all the rewards that society says she should covet: wins, awards, scholarships, recognition, etc. The rewards that most people think define success are actually a by-product of the goal, not the goal itself. Doing her best is the goal. It is all she can do, and it will never be achieved easily. An athlete with a champion's perspective understands that the only time she has any control over for achieving this goal of approaching potential is *right now*. Her goal is to consistently give her best effort one step at a time. The importance of what is next raises her hype level throughout practice. Leaders are intense people.

There are other ways to increase hype level at practice. Remembering how losing felt in the past works wonders for many competitors. Proper goal setting can also help create "pressure." One common goal is to not lose the last game of the year. Other examples include: "I want to run this sprint in under 10 seconds," and "I want to hit my target 75 percent of the time."[17] Adding pressure by having positive incentives for meeting the goals or negative consequences for not meeting them raises the dial further. If making the last play in practice is the difference between picking up the trash and going home to relax, pressure will exist that has similarities to the pressure to make that same play in the game.

---

[17] Chapter 22 addresses the goal setting process in detail.

Finally, an athlete can make practice like performances by using imagery to simulate game experiences. When reality does not allow certain characteristics of the game to be replicated, she can use her imagination to make them feel the same. This works for everyone who has enough imagery skill. It has particular value for hitters. It is difficult to simulate the speed, danger, and variability that a live pitcher poses, so hitters skilled in the use of imagery are simply more prepared than those who are not. Active imagery like a virtual reality game is a great idea, too, but if that is unavailable, she can get her edge with her imagination! No wrong way to practice imagery exists, but the more the athlete's arousal and attitude during vivid imagery reflect the feelings she will experience in the most pressure-filled game conditions, the easier her skills will transfer from practices into those situations.

Figure 13-2

Illusions of Confidence or True Learning

When discussing why we do it that way, leaders are unimpressed by the answer, "Because that's the way it's always been done."

"It is a sad fact that most practice, even at the highest levels of sports, is merely mindless, low grade exercise and not consistent with practices that could be called maximally effective training methods."
—Fran Pirozzolo, Mental Skills Coach

Smart teachers adjust the old saying "practice makes perfect" into "practice makes permanent" or "perfect practice makes perfect." Indeed, practicing a skill wrong will make a person better at doing it wrong. Practice must be designed with quality in mind, as opposed to quantity. Two great repetitions will cause an improvement; 102 bad repetitions will not.

Skill development is not assured just because execution is better after a number of repetitions; true learning requires retention and transfer. This can only be measured by performance at a later time and preferably in the game context. Proficiency at a drill is not the goal; leaders work to get better in the game. Their goal is not to look good, but to be victorious in competition.

For example, some hitters look like superstars hitting the ball hard until they get into the game. Unfortunately, if they do not know how to get their pitch in the game with good timing, this skill in practice will not transfer. There are many great batting practice hitters who cannot hit .250 against decent pitching. Leaders design practice wisely, making sure that it avoids illusions of confidence and leads to positive outcomes against quality competition.

When designing practice, the stage of skill acquisition is important to consider. At the earliest stages, props and aids to indicate how to do something can be very helpful. So can keeping conditions constant. These strategies can be motivational by allowing even more advanced performers to achieve objectives. Unfortunately, they have very little true learning potential beyond the early stages of skill acquisition.

Other practice design issues will directly affect the rate of true learning in the brain. Will skills be practiced in parts or wholes? Making practice like performing requires execution of the whole motor program at once. However, fixing a mechanical flaw can often be best achieved by identifying and working on the precise part that is flawed before integrating the adjustment into the whole movement. Will practice be massed or distributed? Massed practice means repetitions have little or no rest between them, so the motor program does not have to be re-planned on each repetition. For advanced performers, this means that the repetitions after the first one in massed practice often have little or no learning value. If a practice segment will work on skills A, B, and C, will they be blocked (AAA, BBB, CCC) or variable (A, B, C, B, C, A, B, A, C)? Again, the motor programming required to work through the contextual interference within variable practice usually makes it worth the extra effort.

An athlete gets an illusion of confidence when she makes an improvement in practice that is hollow because there is no retention or transfer. Often, she is dependent upon external factors such as a coach's instructions to execute the skill. If she learned new skills, which cannot be truly defined until later, she will be able to execute these skills under pressure and use her learning as part of effective adjustments.

Leaders coach themselves. They know they are good, and they know *why* they are good. They take advantage of coaches and teammates who can help them coach themselves more effectively, but they always try to find answers for themselves first. The mental laziness of dependency on others for answers is foreign to them.

Figure 13-3

Another illusion of confidence forms when the drill is easier than the competitive situation. Batting practice is a prime example, as many hitters want the batting practice pitcher to throw straight balls down the middle of the strike zone at a medium speed. This is, of course, the exact opposite of what the pitcher will be trying to do in the game. A leader does not complain when the batting practice pitcher throws a ball; she appreciates the opportunity to practice her swing decision. She uses variability of practice to enhance learning by encouraging her batting practice pitchers who "mix it up," throwing some pitches slower than what she will face in the game and some harder, or simulate this by moving closer. Also, she does not worry that her confidence will be shot if her last swing of the round did not produce a line drive. Instead of asking for one more pitch, she uses her time between rounds to think about making effective adjustments.

Applying the principles of motor learning (brain pathway development) listed above is not as difficult as it may initially sound. Application to tee work is a great example, and this is also a practice situation that is often made to be too easy. Hitters often practice with the ball placed in the middle of the strike zone, but this will not make her better at hitting the pitches on the corners. However, practicing on (or off) the corners will transfer to improved skill at hitting the ball down the middle. Some hitters will read this and think, "okay, but I just use tee work to get my back loose." Why not loosen up and get better, faster, at the same time? Leaders use tee work to get multiple repetitions practicing the swing that they want to use in the game.

Leaders want to work at and just beyond the edge of their ability level, not well within their comfort zone. They actually practice getting jammed by an inside pitch by putting the tee farther back in their stance than normal. It is not that they want to get jammed, it is that they are realistic and want to have a fighter's chance when inevitable challenges occur. They practice being early on the outside slow pitch by placing the tee outside and forward. They practice hitting offspeed pitches even during tee work by sometimes slightly separating the stride and the swing for all these locations. Also, they take the time to move their feet or the tee so that they can hit the low outside pitch on one swing and the high inside pitch on the next swing. Such a variable practice schedule improves learning. Perhaps they were taught this, but perhaps they just assumed it to be so because they noticed it was harder this way. The logical rule is true: harder is usually better! And by the way… when leaders finish their tee work, their back is loose!

Leaders make practice as much like the game as possible. Scrimmages accomplish this goal fairly well, but there are physical limits and risks that sometimes prohibit scrimmaging. During drills, leaders imagine that it is a scrimmage or "real" game and go game speed. Infielders often imagine a fast batter-runner going down the line so that they will not have to do anything faster than normal when they face the blazing runner in the game. For team defenses, leaders in the infield do not "cheat" while practicing bunt coverages or first and third situations. Even though they know what is going to happen next, they see the play, then react, which causes their decision making to different possibilities to be as close to the same as it will be in the game as possible. Of course, it is impossible to make practice exactly like the game, but leaders strive for perfection by controlling the variables that are available to be controlled.

Leaders are creative and figure out ways to make practice relevant. They use the games to identify weaknesses, and then they design drills to focus on turning those weaknesses into strengths. For example, a hitter notices that she is swinging at pitches she would rather have taken. She also notices that her timing is either early or perfect, but it is seldom late. She uses this information to identify a need for greater patience in the batter's box. Then, she persistently asks, "How do I get more patience?" She might ask teammates, coaches, and the internet. She might study hitters who seem to be good at this skill. She might go stand in the batter's box without a bat while her pitcher teammates are throwing bullpens and have pretend at-bats, really swinging an imaginary bat if appropriate. She could then evaluate her swing decision and timing for this practice. She might try as simple a strategy as saying "be patient" to herself as he final pre-swing thought. She might add a deep breath to her routine just after getting the sign from her third base coach. She will try several of these and other strategies until she notices her timing mistakes are significantly reduced in frequency and half of the mistakes that remain are late.

Leaders learn skills that will serve them in many situations by practicing with a determination to get better, faster. Practice would not be practice to them without attention to details, creativity, and hard work. They work to develop true confidence, not the illusion of confidence that comes from performing an easy drill effectively. They are not satisfied with being good without knowing why they are good. They constantly look for answers about what works so they can repeat it anytime. They get so used to working just beyond the edge of their current skill level that this becomes their norm. They seek out practices that would make others uncomfortable and likely to complain. Of course their attitudes about practice are contagious, so because of their competitiveness and maturity, leaders help build a culture of excellence.

CHAPTER 14

KNOW YOUR JOB TO DO YOUR JOB!

Show class, have pride, and display character. If you do, winning takes care of itself.
—Paul "Bear" Bryant, Football Coach

See the ball, hit the ball.
—Pete Rose, Baseball's All-Time Hits Leader

Many athletes work hard, but do not reach their potential because they are not working smart; they do not have an effective plan of attack. Logically, a good plan is critical. Without it, even a great competitor will flail away with no system for obtaining the outcomes she desires. For example, the athlete who focuses only on winning forgets to focus on *how* to win. Fortunately, the word "w.i.n." is really an acronym designed by geniuses to help athletes understand this concept: What's Important Now.

An effective plan answers the question "What am I trying to do?" In general terms, an athlete's job is always to give her best effort one pitch at a time. Unfortunately, "I want to do my best" does not answer the question of how that will be achieved. Specifics are required. The leader's challenge is to find the goal for this pitch or drill that is as simple as it can be and still be strategically sound. What are her responsibilities? What must she do during this next play to have the best chance of getting a positive outcome? Can she anticipate, or does she need to have patience, reading and reacting to what happens? Or a combination? Is it a good or bad time to go for the lead runner on defense or an extra base on offense? Which is higher, the potential reward or the cost?

The recurring question of a leader is, "What am I trying to do on this pitch?" The answer should be positively stated, as simple as possible while being specific to the situation, and 100 percent controllable. Positivism ensures that the message traveling from the athlete's brain to her body will aid, rather than hinder, her performance. In math, a double negative equals a positive: $-1(-1) = 1$. Softball is not math. Playing not to lose *does not* equal playing to win. Positivism is playing for the love of the game and playing to win. Negative athletic competitors seek to avoid something painful, like losing or looking bad. The difference between the two patterns of thought on performance is huge. Instead of "don't screw up," leaders think "make a play." Instead of "don't strike out," "hit the ball." Instead of "don't walk this batter," "strike her out." Instead of "don't throw it away," "throw it through the first baseman's belly button."

The more the athlete knows about the game, herself, and the opponent, the easier it is to have a plan of attack that is effective *and* simple. The common desire to keep it simple is appropriate in the context of performing, but not appropriate in the context of preparation such as studying an opposing pitcher or understanding the merits of a play's design. An effective plan allows the athlete to keep things simple when it is time for the pitch to occur.

Leaders define their job effectively in large part because they understand what they can control. Chapter 1 discussed the fact that behavior is controllable but outcomes are not. Behavior includes attitude, approach, focus, mechanics, and responses. Athletes reading all the way to here undoubtedly understand that success should not be defined by uncontrollables, but their subconscious mind may not be as well attuned to this truth as it could be.

It is easy to get caught up in focusing on uncontrollable outcomes. An example is often revealed when pitchers are asked what their job is, or how they define success. The most common answers are "to get strikes" or "to get outs." Many times a great pitch does not lead to these goals. Even more often, a poor pitch *does* lead to these goals. Strikes and outs are goals that are too big—they are outside of the pitcher's control. Leaders recognize *how* to give themselves and their teams the best chances for getting strikes and outs. In this case it is quite simple: hit the target aggressively. No matter the situation, consistent pitchers toil by some version of this mantra, "throw the ball aggressively through the target."

Many common answers to the question "What am I trying to do?" are tragically flawed. They are too big or they can be influenced but not controlled. A list of flawed and appropriate answers is shown in Figure 14-1. The "flawed thought" column is filled with appropriate desires, but thinking about these desires will not help the athlete get the job done during the game. Leaders define the process that provides the best statistical chance. This is sometimes obvious, but can also be rather difficult. Softball IQ improves with experience as athletes learn more about themselves and the game. Michael Jordan said about his game, "My roots just kept getting deeper. I dug down deep into the layers of the game. I learned as much as I could about the game, every nuance, every variation. Some trees stop growing and they get blown over in time. I never stopped growing."

Table 14-1

Who	Flawed Goal	Appropriate Thought
Pitcher	Throw a strike	Hit my spot aggressively.
Pitcher	Don't give up a bomb.	Hit my spot aggressively.
Pitcher	Win	Focus one pitch at a time
Hitter	Get a base hit.	Get a good pitch to hit and hit it hard.
Hitter	Hit a home run.	Home runs just happen when I hit the middle of the ball with backspin.
Defender	Make every play.	Make one play: this one.
Infielder	We need the third out.	If a grounder is hit to me, I can throw it to first or second base.
Outfielder	Throw her out at home.	Get behind the ball, see the ball into my glove, and throw the ball through the cutoff.
Baserunner	Take the extra base.	Be aggressive and smart according to the situation.
Baserunner	I gotta get to third base.	Take a chance going for third base because there is one out.
Baserunner	I have to run to the next base so I can score.	Be ready to dive back on a line drive.

The desire to grow like Michael Jordan did throughout his career is a key for continuing to thrive as the competition gets better and better. Kaizen (continuous learning) is the core component of approaching potential. Leaders in sports think like scientists, constantly seeking more knowledge about what works. Coaches typically love to discuss strategic questions, but if a good coach is not available, a determined athlete will find a way to figure out the answers she needs. *"When the pupil is ready, the teacher will appear."* This proverb holds true because the student will constantly be asking the right questions.

Go Fast, Don't Crash

*You've got to have patience and take what's given you.
At the same time, you can't be afraid to pull the trigger.*
—Jerry Bailey, Hall of Fame Jockey

The best, short description of the way any sport should be played is aggressively under control. An analogy with NASCAR clarifies this concept: the accelerator is aggressiveness and the brake is control. Without the accelerator, a driver would not be competitive, but without the brake, she would not be able to finish the race. The challenge that athletes face is finding the appropriate amount of aggressiveness, which is as much as possible without losing control.

How does an athlete find the right amount of aggressiveness? It depends on the person and the situation, but a correct amount always exists. A gymnast competing on the balance beam has a tendency to fall at a specific point of her program. With too much aggressiveness, she falls off to the right. With too little, she falls off to the left. Balance is the goal (both mentally and physically). A hypothetical balance beam exists in every performance situation. Everyone has a tendency to fall off one way or the other in a given situation, as opposed to splitting the mistakes evenly. Awareness of specific situational tendencies enables the athlete to adjust appropriately, so she should always be on the lookout for patterns. Awareness of patterns leads to awareness of personality flaws or tendencies; everyone's personality affects on-field performance in both positive and negative ways. Without awareness, no adjustment to those negative effects is possible.

Control, as in controlled aggression, can be broken down into two component parts: self-control and situational controls. Controlling hype level and emotions is a prerequisite for an athlete to control her performance. To consistently be in control requires a healthy perspective on the game and uncommon levels of awareness and discipline.

Physical balance is indicative of an athlete's self-control or lack thereof. For example, a pitcher or hitter should be explosive, under the control of dynamic balance. If she falls over, even a little, during the pitch or swing, the source of the problem is either insufficiently practiced mechanics or too much aggressiveness. For older players, it is usually the latter. The physical mistake indicates a flaw in the mental approach. Therefore, the solution often lies in adjusting the mental mechanics, not the physical ones.

John Wooden was a great believer in control and balance. For his players, Wooden liked aggressiveness, too, but recognized that competitive athletes are much more likely to lack control than aggressiveness in "big"[18] games. He taught that to remain in control on the basketball court, the student-athlete must be emotionally and spiritually balanced off it. Wooden wrote the following:

> *"I preferred to maintain a gradually increasing level of both achievement and emotions rather than trying to create artificial emotional highs. For every contrived peak you create, there is a subsequent valley. I do not like valleys. Self-control provides emotional stability and fewer valleys."*

Coach Wooden discouraged both excessive celebration and excessive disappointment over outcomes. Instead, his teams were conditioned to play their best ball at the end of games by being prepared physically and mentally. Three specific examples of their preparation follow.

Their stamina was fantastic. Practices were performed at an extremely fast pace, with "move, move, move" being the most common instruction. Wooden made it a point to tell reporters that his players *believed* that they were the best physically conditioned team in the country.

They had the perspective to judge themselves on their effort instead of the score. Some players accepted this lesson more than others during their limited time at UCLA, but it was a lesson that Wooden continually preached so on the whole, his teams understood it better than opposing teams.

Coach Wooden's athletes were in control of themselves. This expectation was standard, regardless of the intensity of the battle being fought. Failure to meet this standard resulted in a lack of playing time. Curse words were not allowed. Wooden wrote:

> *You cannot function physically or mentally unless your emotions are under control. When you lose control of your emotions, when your self-discipline breaks down, your judgment and common sense suffer. How can you perform at your best when you are using poor judgment? Complaining, whining, and making excuses just keeps*

---

[18] Do you know why there are quote marks around the word "big?" It is because success, according to Wooden, is doing your best. That is never more achievable or less achievable. Now is the only time over which we have any control. Restated by Vince Lombardi: "Winning is an all-the-time thing."

> *you out of the present. That's where self-control comes in. Self-control keeps you in the present. Strive to maintain self-control.*

No Doubt

> Commit to a plan of attack. If there is doubt in your mind,
> how can your muscles know what they are expected to do?
> —Harvey Penick, Golf Instructor

> It's better to be decisive than right.
> —Gary Mack, Author and Mental Skills Coach

The second aspect of control in controlled aggression is situational controls. It would be easy to say that an athlete should always "go for the gusto," but she should certainly show restraint at times. It is easy for athletes (who pride themselves on their aggressiveness) to skip the mental discipline required to define situational controls. Leaders are not lazy, and they pride themselves on their superior strategy as well as their athleticism.

As discussed previously, a specific plan of attack is needed in every situation. Sometimes it is better not to go for the extra base. A bunt may be better than swinging away. Throwing to the trail base may be more prudent than throwing to the lead base. A specific plan of attack does not mean that aggressiveness has lost its usefulness. Rather, it means that aggressiveness should be applied to the appropriate strategy.

Athletes must be careful not to be seduced into acting passively by the situational controls, particularly a conservative game plan. On the LPGA tour, if a golfer is leading on the back nine on Sunday by multiple strokes, she should not play conservatively. Rather she should take aggressive swings at conservative targets. Similarly, a sacrifice bunt could be the perfect play call, but it will not work if the players do not aggressively execute it. Some athletes react to a conservative plan from their coach with disappointment. Their belief that the plan is poor turns into a self-fulfilling prophecy because they do not "set the stage" to perform by having an ideal, aggressive attitude. If the athletes do not get themselves ready to perform, no one will ever know if the plan was theoretically solid. They will often think they know, but the experiment they are judging was fixed.

The solution is to play every play the right way: aggressively under control, with commitment to the plan of attack. Commitment means more than a willingness to run the play that is called; it is eagerness. To give her best effort, an athlete must want to do what she is about to do.

When planning strategy, it is often useful to think in global terms that include ramifications of the next play on the long-term goals that the team is trying to achieve. This next play may be designed to set up a big play later on. For example, the 0-2 curve ball away off the plate may set up the 1-2 screwball over the inside corner. Thinking ahead when planning is appropriate, but athletes must remember to refocus back to the task at hand with an aggressive attitude before each pitch happens. Failure to do so, in this pitching situation it was throwing an 0-2 screwball, may lead to a wild pitch or a hard hit ball. Planning is part of the role of coaching, including self-coaching, but athletic execution comes from presentness (see Chapter 17), which requires an absence of too much thinking.

Chapter 15

Success... Guaranteed (Routines)

My thoughts before a big race are pretty simple. I tell myself: "Get out of the blocks, run your race, stay relaxed. If you run your race, you'll win ... Channel your energy. Focus.
—Carl Lewis, Track 17-time Gold Medalist

I don't think I can play any other way than all out. I enjoy the game so much because I am putting so much into it.
—George Brett, Baseball Hall of Famer

The conscious practice of routines leads to the unconscious habits of success. Learn to switch from a thinking mode to a trusting mode.
—Gary Mack, Sport Psychologist and Author

I used to get out there and have a hundred swing thoughts. Now I try not to have any.
—Davis Love III, Golfer

How can an athlete guarantee her best effort during any single performance? What things can she do to ensure that she tries hard, creates her ideal state, commits to an effective plan of attack, and focuses completely on the task at hand? Such a magic formula would have to be different for every person and each performance situation, but a single answer does exist: routines. An athlete's pre-performance routine is her systematic mental and physical preparation for a specific event. It allows her to guarantee that she is doing everything she knows to do at this point in her life to give her best effort on this performance.

The goal of a routine is to set the stage for a best effort performance. A softball player gets her mind ready by using her self-talk to create the attitude from which she performs her best, by committing to a controllable plan of attack, and by making sure that she is not distracted when it is time for the pitch. She gets her body ready by being stretched and ready, energized and relaxed, and aggressive under control. Her routine is a checklist of the steps of her preparation. A leader holds herself accountable for not skipping a step. Her routine is clearly stated, consistently practiced, and adjusted as she learns more about what works best. The routine, then, guarantees that she is in the right place at the right time, to the best of her ability that day. And that, a leader knows, is all *she* can do to give her team the best chance to win the game.

Routines vary greatly in their nature. Almost all professional athletes have a "game day" routine, their countdown to competition. It may start when they wake up, when they arrive at the stadium, when they put their shoes on, or when they go onto the field. Softball is also conducive to a routine for each inning, at-bat, or pitch. It is often possible to observe these pre-performance routines among professional and elite baseball and softball players. Of course, the routine of what is going on inside the athlete's head is invisible. Does she use anchors to create her ideal state quickly? Does she repeat a specific power phrase or use imagery? Perhaps she rehearses a mechanical technique, thinks of a role model, reminds herself of how it felt to lose, or imagines herself making a great play. Whether in preparation to pitch, field, hit, or run, the routine ensures that she is not skipping a step that she might later have regrets about skipping.

Although it may initially seem like using routines during a game leads to a lot of cognitive activity and the possibility of overthinking, quite the opposite is actually the case. To get into the powerful but elusive "trust mode," an athlete must do only two things: have a confident attitude in her approach and focus effectively. Attitudes are controllable by thoughts, and the routine ensures the best thoughts for critical times. To have an effective focus, she must not get in her own way mentally. She must have a quiet mind. The routine for a play is designed to eliminate the chance that her mind will be wandering off in the wrong direction at the wrong time. It makes sure that she keeps things simple.

With commitment and practice, the routine becomes easy to repeat, or routine. It gives athletes something familiar to lean on in potentially uncomfortable situations. With an effective routine, a clear mind at the critical moment of execution becomes habitual, regardless of the "pressure" of the situation. Athletes have routines so they can simply do what they always do, regardless of the changing circumstances. This does wonders for preventing the hype level from being too high or too low. Such thorough preparation also increases confidence.

The most important pitch in the game is the next one. It is the only one an athlete can control, the only one that concerning herself with is useful for enhancing performance. (This statement is always true about athletic execution; strategy formation is a separate topic.) Unfortunately, this mature focus on the task at hand is extremely difficult, even though the concepts involved are quite simple. Leaders use their routines to ensure, rather than hope, that the goal of playing the game one pitch at a time is met.

Ken Ravizza and Tom Hanson outlined their book, *Heads-Up Baseball: Playing the Game One Pitch at a Time*, around the control-plan-trust model for a pitch. It tells athletes to first make sure that they have emotional *control* of themselves. Next, *plan*. Athletes must know the job to be done on this play, forming a specific and controllable plan of attack. Finally, they should get into a *trust* mode and let it happen.

In this model, control means self-control: a "green light" performance state from the traffic light analogy. As an athlete gains experience checking her traffic light, doing so becomes more and more routine. Eventually, the check is automatic in normal circumstances, as a "yellow light" or "red light" feels wrong, alerting her to pause and gather. In special circumstances, she will quickly check to make sure that her extra adrenaline and excitement are working for her, rather than allowing her nerves to lead to a loss of control.

Figure 15-1

Ideal and consistent self-control is elusive, which is why John Wooden's consistent modeling of self-control and his persistence in teaching that the game is mostly fought between the ears gave his teams an edge. His players probably stayed under control better than others because he worked so hard to convince them that as long as they were giving their best effort, they deserved to have peace of mind. Wooden also reminded them often to maintain emotional balance, avoiding both the peaks and the valleys that are all too common in athletics.

Arriving at the time of the pitch in a trust mode is an elusive goal. Both attitude and focus are completely within the control of every athlete, though mastering either is obviously difficult. It should be every athlete's goal to anchor (next chapter) a trusting state at game time. Then, focus appropriately by knowing what to look at and mentally staying out of the way. The superior athlete does not have any "paralysis by analysis." Finding a trust mode on command is easy to say and tough to execute, but this is great news for competitors. If it was easy, everyone would do it well and less opportunity would exist to gain an edge by training mental skills.

Example Routine – Throwing a Pitch

1. **Do not engage the rubber until attitude is positive and focus is present.**
2. **What pitch and what specific location**
3. **Breath**
4. **Image (typically the last six feet of the ball doing what you want it to do as it goes into the catcher's mitt)**
5. **Target (Tunnel-vision focus during the delivery)**

Example Routine – Baserunning

1. **Celebrate**
2. **S.o.s – Get the 'S'ignal**
3. **s.O.s. – Know the 'O'uts – Be particularly aggressive getting to second base or home with two outs, and to third base with one out.**
4. **s.o.S. – Know the 'S'ituation**
5. **Check defensive positioning, starting with the outfielders**
6. **Remind self to be ready for a wild pitch/passed ball and a line drive (if less than two outs). Be particularly ready to dive back if the line drive is hit near you where a double play could happen quickly[19].**
7. **Take a deep breath**
8. **Read and react to what you see (avoid anticipating)**

---

[19] Author's pet peeve: a baserunner gets doubled off on a line drive and then says, implies, or is told by teammates that it was not her fault: "Wow, that stinks. Nothing you can do." Leaders are great baserunners who appreciate the value of each of the three outs in a half-inning.

Example Routine – an At-Bat
1. Get ready, including getting loose. Lots of preparation happens before you are in the hole, but putting on the helmet and batting gloves could be considered the start of the routine.
2. On deck, practice timing your stride and seeing the ball well right from the release point.
3. Imagery snapshot of your Personal Past Peak Performance as you leave the on-deck circle.
4. Think, "This is a great opportunity to…" while getting the batter's box dirt comfortable.
5. Get the sign from the third base coach.
6. Commit to a plan that defines what pitches to swing at and where to try to hit/bunt/slap them.
7. Take a focal breath, staring at a small spot on your bat while feeling a comfortable deep breath. Repeat this step if the spot is not in focus or the breath is choppy.
8. Step into the box with a "Yes, yes, yes – I'm going to swing at my pitch" aggressive mentality. You've already defined what pitches you will take, so your brain does not need to get involved anymore. Your eyes will tell your body not to swing if the pitch is outside your "yes" zone.
9. Affirm: "Just do what I do."
10. Image a line drive with backspin exploding into the opposite field gap as you take a few loose, easy, rhythm swings.
11. As the pitcher is about to begin her wind-up, your mind goes quiet and your eyes go to her throwing-side hip, then the release point[20].

---

[20] Most hitters do not repeat this routine every pitch. Rather, they do it before the first pitch, a couple appropriate parts every pitch, and repeat it in its entirety if something happens during the AB that bothers them. Examples could be a bad call by the umpire or fouling a fat pitch straight back. In this case, add a "flushing" mechanism before restarting the routine.

Chapter 16

Instant Improvement (Anchoring)

Having a choice is better than not having a choice.

You can change state in an instant.
—Anthony Robbins, Motivational Guru

If I would be happy, I would be a very bad ballplayer.
With me, when I get mad, it puts energy in my body.
—Roberto Clemente, Baseball Hall of Famer

At sea, an anchor is something a sailor throws down to make sure that she stays in the correct place, rather than drifting off in a potentially damaging direction. In life, failure to manage the mind can lead to both attitudes and behaviors drifting off in damaging directions. The body, too, may not be cooperating. The fear of failure is often manifested in very physical ways. Stress causes tension, shallow breathing, discomfort, and more. Most solutions take time, but one quick-fix exists: using anchors to instantly connect the mind and body to where the athlete wants them to be. Athletes have many anchors already and can build more if they know how and are properly motivated. An anchor is the athlete's quick fix tool for changing her internal state.

An anchor is a representation or stimulus that triggers a specific response in the brain, such as a particular attitude and physiological state. It is more than just a reminder or cue, though cues can have great value for athletes by themselves. An anchor is more; it is an actual connection in the brain between a unique stimulus and a unique response. Both good and bad anchors already exist in every person, other than babies. Advertisers pay good money to build anchors, planting the seeds that make us have a Big Mac attack, get milk (it does a body good), or buy Nike shoes (just do it). Leaders build new anchors, designing them to provide what they need when they need it. It may build confidence, block a negative or distracting thought, aid relaxation, promote the ideal hype level, or initiate a laser-like focus on the task at hand. A well-designed anchor can turn a huge "red light" to "green" in an instant.

Leaders either build anchors or identify existing ones that are helpful and can be used on command. Executing either strategy is unnatural. Therefore, most people do neither. A leader is so excited by the quick-fix power of anchors that she is sufficiently motivated to get out of her comfort zone and work on building and using anchors.

Anchors can take many forms; each athlete should pick the ones that make sense to her, using these guidelines. Each anchor should be special: something distinct from everyday movements, sounds, or pictures. The anchor is not something that she would ever want to ignore. Also, she must make sure that it will be available when it is needed, whether she is in familiar environs or not.

Figure 16-1

Anchors can be kinesthetic, like hand gestures. Making the "ok" sign with the thumb and forefinger and moving it a certain way is one example. Tapping the thumb and middle finger fingertips in both hands is another. The hand motion that simulates chopping wood (right-hand karate chops into open left palm) was an anchor for the entire Rutgers Football team in 2006. Their coach, Greg Schiano, had instilled in them the importance of consistent hard work. He created a link for the team during a team-building exercise in which this anchor created the determination needed to keep working hard. If things are bad, keep chopping wood. If things are good, keep chopping wood. Anytime Coach Schiano wanted to remind her players to avoid excuses and have a determined attitude on this next play, he would simply pretend to chop wood.

Anchors can be auditory, like a favorite song. Many athletes wear headphones during their countdown to competition. A favorite song, sound, voice, and set of words in self-talk or aloud can all be anchors. The sound of a bell was an anchor for Pavlov's dogs. When they heard the bell, the dogs instantly went into a state of salivation and anticipation. Former NFL placekicker and scratch golfer Al Del Greco used the word "birdie" immediately before every kick because, for him, this word anchored a carefree mood, having fun, and being confident.

Anchors can be visual. A hitter may stare at the ball for five seconds before each at-bat, linking her brain to an effective external/narrow focus. Entire teams sometimes place a safety pin with a school-colored tag among their shoelaces. Each time a player sees it, which may happen particularly when she is tired or feeling (and looking) down, she is filled with school pride and empowered with energy and determination to do her job. Of course, these only work if the anchors were properly built. Many Americans use Old Glory to feel humbled and appreciative. The flag communicates appreciation for the awesome opportunities Americans are given.

Athletes can use imagery as anchors. An athlete is a complex person with many significant memories. She can search her soul to find the memories that generate the enthusiasm, toughness, focus, or calmness she seeks. An image of a particular person, a past experience, a movie scene, or any imagined experience can all be anchors. As suggested in the exercise above, these special images can be used during a longer imagery session during her pre-game routine or as brief snapshots of that same scene during competition.

EXERCISE

Think of your P.P.P.P. (personal, past, peak performance). Pick out a long version and short version of that memory. Practice imaging the long version in detail so that you re-experience the feelings you had when this happened. When you feel it, link this feeling to a unique movement. Next, learn to create those same feelings with the short version, a snapshot of this past peak performance. Again, link the confident and specific feelings you had that day with the unique movement. Next, reinforce the anchor by imaging the snapshot and doing the movement when you already have the feeling it is designed to generate. Finally, use it or lose it. Practice dropping your anchor (snapshot and movement) in your pre-game and gathering routines.

Building a new anchor takes several steps. First, define the desired positive state to be reached. Second, pick the anchor: internal or external, verbal, visual, or kinesthetic. Third, image an experience to produce that ideal state *and* feel it strongly. When the desired internal state is achieved, throw anchor by doing the selected trigger. Strengthen the anchor by repeating the trigger anytime the desired state is achieved, whether by real or imagined experiences. Once the anchor is set, use it or lose it.

Anchors can prevent the other team from getting a full-throttled rush of momentum because momentum is an attitude, a simple expectation of great outcomes on the next few plays. After a big play by one team, the other team's attitude often suffers. Their disappointment compounds the problem of the big play, and the snowball effect begins for both teams: one positive and one negative. Any time the negative snowball effect is beginning is a good time to drop anchor. If players know where to go mentally, they can avoid a letdown and continue to play up to their potential, releasing the disappointment of the last play and doing their jobs on the next play with an expectation of success.

Steps to Build an Anchor

1. Be clear and specific about the positive internal state you want to be able to create.
2. Pick the distinct cue that will become your anchor (kinesthetic, power phrase, visual, auditory, or imagined).
3. Recall a specific time when you were firmly in that state or think of a time when you will be there.
4. Image that experience vividly.
5. When you have the feeling you want, drop anchor.
6. Practice dropping your anchor. You will either use it or lose it.
7. Reinforce the anchor by repeating it when you find yourself firmly in the state that it is designed to create.

PART 4:

GO! TIME

When I go out on the ice, I just think about my skating. I forget it is a competition.
—Katarina Witt, Olympic Gold Medalist

What I know is that when you are in the process, you are not playing for the reward. That releases your talent. That releases your energy. That releases your potential.
—Augie Garrido, Baseball Coach

Once the athlete is ready and set, it is time to go! A priority for leaders is to get lost in the process of performing by focusing completely on the task at hand. This section provides details and distinctions about what it means to focus effectively one pitch at a time… and how to do it.

In the movie *For Love of the Game*, Kevin Costner played a pitcher who said, "Clear the mechanism." This phrase was his anchor for blocking out distractions and locking his mind onto the task at hand. It gave him tunnel vision. Hank Aaron blocked out distractions when he was sitting on the bench by covering his face with his hat and staring at the pitcher through the little eyelet. Whatever the sport and whoever the athlete, focus is a common variable for every successful performance.

All athletes think too much at times. Most recognize this as a mistake. They have also experienced being totally engrossed in the moment and recognize this as a powerful feeling that they want to repeat. Leaders make developing the skill to focus with tunnel vision on the task at hand a priority. Some are naturally good at it. For others, it is very much a learned skill. Whether it is in their first or second nature, leaders know how to switch back and forth between being an athlete and being a coach. Between pitches, they coach, caring for themselves and teammates. When it is time for athletic action, they are neither analyzing nor caring. Rather, they are looking at a target and playing the game. Leaders may have even more potential distractions than others, but they are exceptional at blocking them out. When it is time to perform, they focus on doing their job to the best of their ability.

CHAPTER 17

THE NOW

If you play the game like that—one pitch, one hitter, one inning at a time—the next thing you know you look up and you've won.
—Rick Dempsey, Baseball Player

It's all about executing a pitch.
—Greg Maddux, Baseball Hall of Famer

In January of 2012, Alabama and LSU played for the second time that season for a national championship. LSU was undefeated, thanks in part to defeating Alabama 6-3 during the regular season. LSU was a slight favorite, but Alabama won 21-0. After the game, the interview moderator asked Alabama Head Coach Nick Saban,

> *Nick, this movie that you guys went to see last night sounds a little like a variation on what you've been saying all year about finish, finish, finish. In this game, did you feel like this team came as close as a team can come to finishing every play mentally, physically, and emotionally?*

Coach Saban replied,

> *That was kind of the message before the game -- that we wanted to finish. In fact, it was a question: How bad do you want to finish? What's your effort going to be, your enthusiasm, your excitement to play in the game, the toughness that you're willing to play with, all the intangibles? You do all that one play at a time, regardless of what happens in the game. And I think that was key. We certainly didn't play a perfect game. We got a field goal blocked. We couldn't score a touchdown for a long time. But the guys just kept playing and never once was anybody ever discouraged about anything that happened in the game. And I think that attitude prevailed for us as a team. We were just going to play one play at a time and finish each play. And regardless of what the circumstance was on the play*

> *before, have a sort of an 'I will not be denied' attitude about how to play the next play. And I think that that spirit was reflected out there in the way our players competed.*

Presentness is the ability to be completely engrossed in the now. When performing, the task at hand is the only thing that matters. "Know your job; do your job." "Task. Task. Task." "One play at a time." "Execute." "Make a play." In all its simplicity, this mantra is critical, however it is worded. An athlete's consistency is defined by her ability to give her best effort one time, deal with whatever happens, and repeat. She maximizes her consistency by controlling the controllables in each pitch's approach, focus, and response.

Humans are capable of processing literally thousands of thoughts per minute. They can concern themselves with the past, the future, or the various things going on right now. Often, it is useful to think about many different things. Performance time is not one of these times. The leader's goal is to lose herself in the process of doing her job. Her concentration cannot be ideal if any part of her mind is distracted by thoughts about the past or the future. She stays in the moment by setting aside her needs, fears, desires, satisfactions, and regrets. Only the now is controllable.

A singular focus on the task at hand happens at very specific times on the diamond. A hitter steps into the batter's box with both feet. A pitcher engages the pitching rubber. A baserunner positions her body to leave base at (or just before) the release of the pitch. A defender other than the pitcher steps forward on to the balls of her feet. Often, an athlete will try hard and perform lousy because of her inability to be fully present. Being totally engrossed in the softball experience is empowering and loads of fun, but is it a skill that can be practiced? Absolutely!

Focusing completely on one thing at a time can be difficult. A common hindrance is worry about what teammates, coaches, and parents will think. It is wonderful to want to please others, but being a "people pleaser" is a common personality flaw when it comes to focusing on the task at hand. Leaders work to please themselves, trusting that doing so maximizes their chances at pleasing others.

When the hero of the game is asked afterwards how she was able to come through in big spots, a common refrain is "I was just trying to be in the moment." Well, is it not true that everyone is living in the moment? Yes…physically, but not mentally. Many athletes do not know how to release regrets or block out worries. Even though it is outside of their ability to express control over anything other than what is happening now, they waste some attention on the past or future.

During the game, the next play is all that matters and awareness is always the first step to making effective adjustments. Certain words and ideas are warning signals. Bad thoughts like, "I need to make a play" indicate that worry exists. "Need," "gotta," and "have to" communicate a fear that if the good outcome does not happen soon, a horrible future will result! Simply replace these "curse" words with "want." Similarly, replace "should" and "supposed to" with "will" "can" or "could."

Figure 17-1

There is a time to analyze, but when performing, leaders release any regrets, grudges, or even questions about the past. They even let go of positive thoughts about the past. Other athletes think they are doing well with the thought, "I can't believe I messed that up. I won't do that again." This may lead to a good adjustment between pitches, but if it remains in consciousness when it is time for the pitch, this thought interferes with an effective focus.

John Wooden said success is "the peace of mind that is a direct result of self-satisfaction in knowing you did your best to become the best you are capable of becoming." Athletes who completely agree have a competitive advantage in that they are skilled at focusing on the task at hand. Now. Without peace of mind, some fear (worry) about the future will inevitably intrude upon consciousness at just the wrong time. But perhaps even more common than worrying about the future is holding onto regrets about the past, so leaders use their mental skills to…

Flush the "Poop"

Adversity is inevitable. Snowballing mistakes are not.

I can forgive, but I cannot forget, is only another way of saying, I will not forgive.
-Henry Ward Beecher, 19th Century American Preacher and Political Leader

An athlete does not need to be perfect to be mentally tough, but she must know how to keep a mistake on one play from having a negative effect on a future play. Inevitably, some "poop" will hit the fan. How does she "flush" the past and get that "poop" –negative and distracting thoughts– out of her head? By focusing on the plan and execution of the next play. A great mantra for athletes: "Flush it! What's next?" If practiced often enough, executing this plan becomes second nature. Many athletes do a version of this, but lack clarity about their own strategy. Adding clarity and practicing this skill of forgetting bad stuff by focusing on their job on the next play ingrains this good habit.

Very few athletes have mastered "flushing" it. Sometimes, the attempt to forget the past is unsuccessful. When the athlete is frustrated and the memory is stuck in consciousness, a second strategy is needed. In other words, it is common that an athlete might hold onto negative emotions about the umpire's call, the teammate's mistake, or the fact that she just messed something up that she normally can do perfectly 10 of 10 times in practice. The single key that will allow her to "flush it" when the "poop" is stuck is (drum roll, please)… forgiveness.

Why should an athlete forgive a mistake or bad luck? Two answers are needed: because if she does not do so, she will probably not let it go. Many athletes understand this first answer readily, but are still commonly unable to forgive because they forget the other reason: nobody is perfect.

Why should I forgive myself for messing up?

1. If I don't, I will be likely to "snowball" my mistakes.
2. Nobody is perfect.

Doesn't this risk acceptance of mediocrity?

Yes, so remember to strive for perfection without ever expecting it.

Accepting that all people are flawed and going to make mistakes on the field does not mean that it is okay to make mistakes. True, all humans are flawed so forgiveness is wise, but it is also a mark or a champion to keep pushing forward. Coach Wooden knew how to balance out these seemingly contradictory ideas. He taught one of this book's favorite motifs: "Strive for perfection, but never expect it."

Leaders make it a priority to nurture three traits within the culture of their teams: enthusiasm, excellence, and forgiveness. The first two are common goals within serious teams, but the importance of forgiveness for consistency is often underappreciated. Having both excellence and forgiveness as priorities strikes the balance of consistently pushing forward without losing emotional control when mistakes inevitably occur. And without forgiveness, mistakes make the goal of enthusiasm impossible to maintain.

EXERCISE

Pick a partner and hold each other accountable for flushing the past. Each person picks a visible "flushing" motion that they will do to cue the idea of getting completely focused on what is next. Examples include sweeping away the past with a foot, tossing it aside, brushing it off your shoulder, or taking off your helmet to let it float away.

When you or someone around you makes a mistake, think, "Great, now I can practice forgiving to forget!" Next, make your chosen "flushing" motion to indicate you have let it go. Remember to forgive first, then "flush" it. Watch out for your partner during practices and games to make sure she is not missing an opportunity to practice this skill. It is common to act emotionally rather than rationally when the "flushing" is called for, so the partner part of this exercise is likely to improve awareness, giving you an edge over your competition! Together, you and your teammates can form great habits of playing the game one pitch at a time.

Don't Try Harder, Try Easier

> The greatest efforts in sports come when the mind is as still as a glass lake.
> —Tim Gallwey, Author

> The thing I had on my side was patience.
> —Hank Aaron, Baseball Hall of Famer

> You can want it too much. You can try too hard.
> —Carol Heiss Jenkins, Olympic Champion Skater

A physical manifestation of the wrong mental attitude is tightness. Over-muscling, or pressing, is self-defeating but common when an athlete fails to find her trusting attitude. The prepared, confident, enthusiastic, brave, respectful athlete can relax; she feels no need to "muscle up" to get the job done. She is confident that she already has enough "juice" to succeed, in part because she knows that all she can do is all she can do. It is also all she needs to do to be successful. Leaders define success, then, not by beating the opponent, but by beating the obstacles she faces for a best effort performance. They try easy and allow great outcomes to come as they will.

Upon reaching a reasonably high level of play, most athletes are familiar with the usefulness of staying within themselves, but few are taught how to do this. They want to make it happen, rather than allowing it to. Awareness, as usual, is the first step. Athletes should understand not only the value of letting the game come to them, but also the reasons that this is typically so tough to do. This book attempts to address many of them. In other words, all mental skills training is designed to help athletes develop a healthy perspective on the game and gathering strategies to get themselves centered so they can let their game flow.

Leaders trust both themselves and the idea that, in the long run, outcomes will occur as they should even though short-run outcomes often are not fair. The "trust" phase of the "control-plan-trust" routine could be considered the most critical phase because it includes the time when the action occurs. Because it is a culmination of all work done in both physical and mental preparation, trusting it can seem both complicated and difficult. It is actually easy to say and understand; it is just difficult to do it. Leaders are willing and even eager to do what is difficult. Since most athletes do not share this eagerness for challenges and struggles, this gives them an edge over their competition.

When an athlete gets in her own way by thinking too much rather than focusing with tunnel vision, she is often chasing the game rather than letting it flow to her.

Phrases that reflect this critical concept include "let it happen," "trust yourself," "stay within yourself," or "my best effort is always good enough." Assuming that the athlete does know what to focus her attention on, her focus will be excellent when she trusts her stuff. Instead of trying too hard, she will try easy.

The idea of not trying too hard may, at first, seem like an oxymoron. Athletes frequently hear about how much they have to "want it" to be successful. Indeed, this concept is true, so trying to make things happen is a normal response of "wanting it" very much. But Michael Jordan warns that one of the differences between a good athlete and a great one is that the great one lets the game come to her instead of chasing it. Make no mistake about it, the gap between good and great is huge. However, getting there may be as simple as learning to stop chasing success and letting it happen.

Leaders prepare and focus extremely well, making their superb performances appear easy. This appearance is deceiving; it is never easy to give a best effort performance. Their dedication to developing their physical and mental skills allows them to excel. With high self-esteem, their priorities in order, and through the use of effective patterns of self-talk, they have learned to have the right attitude at the right time. Even in circumstances that would make most people tight and uncomfortable, leaders relax and focus on executing their plan of attack. Through the process of giving their best effort one step at a time, they let success happen.

Chapter 18

Fine Focus

*Concentrate all your thoughts upon the work at hand.
The sun's rays do not burn until brought to a focus.*
—Alexander Graham Bell, Inventor

Tunnel vision is how I explain it. You become isolated from all outside distraction…and there's only you… and the catcher. It's the most satisfying feeling I've known.
—Nolan Ryan, Baseball Hall of Famer

Concentration and dedication—the intangibles—are the deciding factors between who won and who lost.
—Tom Seaver, Baseball Hall of Famer

Courage means being afraid to do something, but still doing it.
—Knute Rockne, Football Coach

Concentration is the secret of strength in politics, in war, in trade, in short, in all the management of human affairs.
—Ralph Waldo Emerson, Poet

Great concentration and focus are behaviors that coaches ask for often. Unfortunately, strategies for improving these skills can be difficult to identify. Webster's defines the act of concentrating as "directing attention toward a single objective, or to focus." It is something that cannot be forced, but neither is it appropriate just to wait and hope for it to happen.

Concentration is a skill, and skills improve with practice. Figure 18-1 provides a fun way to practice concentration, and infinite other opportunities also exist. In fact, every time an athlete knows she did something right, she did it with good concentration. If she has doubt, her concentration could improve. With practice, superb concentration can become a habit. Greg Maddux learned to concentrate exclusively on the next pitch so routinely that he said, "I can't do it wrong anymore."

Figure 18-1: Concentration Exercise

> **Directions:** Mark a line through each number starting with 00 and going as high as possible in a set amount of time. To re-use, do it backward, or start at a different number. For an advanced version, add potential distractions such as music or talking.

17	61	25	85	07	77	04	68	65	80
76	40	92	16	53	27	28	34	90	84
59	55	13	15	70	48	03	44	89	23
50	51	66	33	09	01	71	10	32	52
38	45	74	43	60	95	20	72	26	06
88	31	46	99	19	82	78	22	97	91
93	05	58	96	83	12	81	21	41	14
49	56	64	35	94	73	63	18	69	47
36	79	42	29	87	37	00	02	39	57
54	11	75	86	24	98	67	62	08	30

Concentration and focus are similar in meaning, but it is possible to have great concentration and horrible focus on the task at hand because the concentration is misguided. Concentrating on inappropriate stimuli will have the expected effect of hindering performance. Thus, it is important to "know your job," including what to focus on, before trying to "do your job."

Perspective was explained earlier as having an overall set of priorities and a specific way of looking at things. The latter part refers to how closely an athlete is looking at something and from what angle. A picture across the room appears much different than if it is an inch away. It looks different still if the athlete is a part of the picture, looking at it from within the frame.

In performance, it is important for an athlete to know how closely to look at the picture. When it is time to perform on the diamond, keep it small. The inability to zero in on appropriate cues at the critical time of performance limits many performances. Peak performers have "tunnel vision," where the world all around the task at hand seems to fade out. It is still there, but it is not currently relevant so it is not attended to. The brain is trained to block that information from consciousness. Tunnel vision can cause the target to actually appear larger than normal and can make time seem to slow down, though of course it does not.

Low self-esteem limits performance by keeping an athlete from actualizing the person she is capable of becoming. Failing to resolve personal issues prevents growth in self-esteem. Depending on the situation, the best way to keep off-the-field issues from affecting a performance may be to battle them with determination and honesty, similar to how an athlete would fight to overcome a weakness in her physical skills. This can be more painful than a physical injury. Courage is required.

Figure 18-2

Courage is the strength of will to do what is difficult. When courage and motivation are combined, mountains will be overcome one step at a time, and then look like molehills in the distance behind. Without courage, even a molehill is insurmountable. With courage, an ingrown toenail is irrelevant during a performance. Without courage, the injured athlete loses intensity, focus, and balance. Without courage, adversity is bad and represents the end of the road. With courage, adversity is actually sought out because mistakes are viewed as critical components for growth and happiness. With the courage to admit mistakes, weaknesses become strengths. Without it, weaknesses continue unabated or even grow until they eventually blow up. With courage, leaders create new habits, turning weaknesses into strengths. They form the powerful habit of making excellence second nature.

Without courage, athletes make excuses. Without courage, the fear of failure can debilitate. With it, fear helps athletes reach new heights of personal or human achievement because courage reveals fear and pressure for what they really are: the shadows of great opportunities. This is why Winston Churchill said, "Without courage, all other virtues lose their meaning." If motivation and courage are sufficient, the athlete will find a way to get her job done.

Some people are unable or afraid to battle their personal issues at this time, making the skill of concentration even more critical and powerful. If an athlete's concentration is superb, even unresolved difficulties in her life *might* not interfere with her focus and performance. These outside issues are temporarily blocked from causing problems. Many athletes use the playing field as a refuge. They recognize that nothing can be accomplished by worrying about these problems while they are playing the game, so they enjoy losing themselves in their sport for a few hours.

> **Moral Courage** – The strength of will to do what is emotionally difficult, even in the face of peer pressure or personal weaknesses. It risks embarrassment and "failure." Its beneficiaries: your peace of mind / self-esteem and your team.

Attend-WHAT? (Dimensions of Attentional Control)

> Concentration is the ability to think about absolutely nothing
> when it is absolutely necessary.
> —Ray Knight, Baseball Player

> You don't aim at the bull's-eye. You aim at the center of the bull's-eye.
> —Raymond Berry, Football Coach

Four dimensions of attentional control exist that come from two domains: width and locus. Width can be broad or narrow; locus is in relation to oneself: either internal or external.

These dimensions of focus are easily understood with examples. A broad-internal focus is thinking about a person's internal state, meaning all details of attitude and physiology. To review, attitude is a function of thoughts and physiology is a function of many factors, led by body language. A leader knows her traffic light signals, remembers to check them appropriately, and knows how to make the light "green" again when it is yellow or red.

Figure 18-3

	External		
Broad	Assess the situation	Perform a skill	Narrow
	Analyze internal state	Rehearse mechanics	
	Internal		

A narrow-internal focus means a person is thinking about a particular muscle group or rehearsing a specific mechanical objective. Examples include focused stretching, staying low, or keeping the elbows in their proper position. Much of coaching is done with this type of focus in mind, and creating proper mechanics and muscle memory is a critical step of preparation. Athletes must remember, however, that at the time of performance, a narrow-internal focus is a significant distraction from an ideal (narrow, external) focus on the task at hand.

An example of a broad-external focus is assessing the situation. Softball players assess by knowing the score, outs, and situation, the play call, and checking their opponents' positioning, setup, or actions. Leaders transition from a broad-external focus to a narrow-external one shortly before each pitch. This is often not an instantaneous transition, but can be thought of a narrowing process ending with laser-like intense focus on.

A narrow-external focus is looking at something small such as a target or the ball. This is where athletes often want to be when it is time to perform. Tasks such as pitching and hitting are performed better with this singular focus. Leaders have a consistent goal of being focused in this way for every pitch. They do not deviate from this goal, though they will face many temptations and distractions.

In reviewing the control-plan-trust routine, it is noteworthy that this model is actually a guide for having the correct type of attentional focus at the correct time. Begin with a broad-internal focus to create an ideal state, go to a broad-external focus and formulate a plan of attack, and then trust it and as the play develops, narrow in and see the target big.

CHAPTER 19

PRESSURE: YES, COLLAPSE: NO

Under pressure you can perform fifteen percent better or worse.
—Scott Hamilton, Olympic Figure Skater

The only pressure I'm under is the pressure I've put on myself.
—Mark Messier, Hockey Hall of Famer

Pressure is something you feel when you don't know what the hell you're doing.
—Peyton Manning, Quarterback

Heart in champions has to do with the depth of your motivation and how well your mind
and body react to pressure—that is, being able to do what you do best
under maximum pain and stress.
—Bill Russell, Basketball Hall of Famer

It is undeniable that pressure can cause a collapse. Pump the air out of an empty, plastic container and it will crumble. Nothing is inside the container to resist the normal air pressure on the outside. Internal resistance is necessary for the container to maintain its integrity because at least some pressure always exists on the outside.

People can crumble just like plastic containers. Such a collapse is sometimes called "choking," but terminology is not the point here. Consistency is the point. Numerous pressures are always present, but athletes who have the mental skills needed to handle them maintain their integrity. They remain whole. An athlete who maintains her integrity will perform up to her potential.

A leader's singular goal is that she and her teammates perform at or near their best. She does not expect more, and she does not accept less. The relevant question, then, is not how much pressure a situation presents but how much resistance the athlete needs to deal with that pressure, and how much does she have. Resistance equals skills developed through preparation. An athlete who is physically and mentally prepared will handle pressure effectively. The situation will not keep her from giving her best effort. Similarly, pressure could seem to be minimal, but if there is a deficiency of physical or mental skills, a collapse will occur.

Please consider yet again John Wooden's definition of success: "the peace of mind that comes from knowing you did your best." This peace of mind represents the exact opposite of feeling pressure, the opposite of worry. A leader would never feel *more* pressure if her *only* goal was to do her best[21]. She would pursue this goal constantly and know that achieving it maximizes her chances of winning, getting awards, looking good, not looking stupid, etc. She would consistently feel pressure to do her best, even in practice. The amount would not change, which is why she places the word "clutch" in quotation marks. No situation is more important than others. The only performance that can impact her top goal is the one she is giving right now, whether right now is during practice, a "boring" game, an "easy" matchup, a "big" game, or the "do or die" moment at the end of a playoff game. Restated: the leader does not care less about these "special" situations. She cares more about all the other situations.

With this philosophy, pressure still exists, but it is constant and routine. Dramatic moments add excitement and adrenaline, but they are not accompanied by the typical loss of self-control. The degree to which a person wants to win (or make money or achieve any other outcome) more than do her best is directly proportional to how much more pressure she will have to cope with in "important" situations.

Most elite softball players' careers go through similar stages. In youth leagues, they are the best players, physically, and there are not that many challenges to their mental foundational skills. At some point they decide that now softball matters. They start to press. They lose the "green" light carefree, enthusiastic attitude that has always been there before. They lack awareness and get confused about why they are struggling. Then, one of two things happens. This separates leaders from others. They either gain awareness and adjust, or they do not.

Since very few athletes *completely* accept Wooden's definition of success in American society, it is useful to expand this discussion. Consider the general sources of pressure. Internal pressures are within the athlete, and external pressures are all others, such as the need to please others and earn awards. External sources only exert as much pressure as each athlete allows them to, so ultimately, the pressure any athlete feels is her responsibility.

---

[21] Getting to this singularity of purpose is great to strive for, even if achieving it is unrealistic for most people in America's competitive (with others) culture. The closer the leader gets, the more she will practice with intensity and perform up to her potential in "clutch" situations.

Two models of the way pressure impacts performance are possible, but only one is always true. The bottom model shown in Figure 19-1 is always true and is preferable because it allows some potentially strong external pressures to be diffused by the athlete because she feels only the pressure she is placing on herself. Unfortunately, many people allow the top model to equal the bottom model in its effect. They do not think in a way that diffuses the way they feel about external pressures. They do not bring a healthy perspective with them to game day.

Figure 19-1

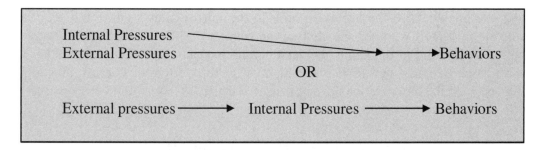

Two ways exist to minimize the negative effects of pressure: reduce the external pressure or increase the internal resistance. Strategies for diminishing external pressures include an acceptance of responsibility and the maintenance of a healthy perspective. An athlete with these strategies has successfully converted the top model in Figure 19-1 into the bottom model. Coping mechanisms for dealing effectively with internal pressures provide the needed resistance to maintain integrity and play up to potential. They primarily include the mental skills of self-control and focus, though realistically they include all mental skills.

The way an athlete interprets a situation can dramatically affect how much outside pressure she feels. If she is not dependent on good outcomes to feel good about herself, she will feel less pressure. Acceptance of responsibility puts the ball in an athlete's court, preventing her from feeling (and acting) helpless. Once she has accepted responsibility, she hunts for an effective definition of her job. If she often crumbles under the pressure, then she likely has an unhealthy view of the situation, thinking that outside forces are making things unfair or unmanageably difficult. She should, instead, figure out a way to focus on controllable variables. Whatever the situation, a job for her exists that is completely controllable and anyone who asks an athlete to do more than what she can control is obviously making an inappropriate request. Athletes who define success as Wooden did find it easy to focus on controllable variables.

Any "tough" situation can be viewed as a challenge to meet or a threat of defeat. More pressure equals more opportunity! A healthy perspective is to focus on the opportunities that this challenge presents! Leaders recognize that the worst outcome imaginable from this situation is *not* a catastrophe and that it would not define or even affect their value as people. They coach themselves to create an ideal performance state, and then they define their controllable job in specific yet simple terms. Finally, they stop being a coach and become an athlete focused on the task at hand. They deal with pressure by systematically giving their best effort one pitch at a time.

Does the pitcher have the ability to look in the mirror after a game and feel the same about herself whether she gave up no runs or 10? Does she have no regrets about what she did in the game? Understanding that outcomes do not define her is difficult, particularly before her self-identity is fully formed. Factors in young athletes' socialization create a normal fear of "failure."

Fear of Failure: Universal and Good

Some people think that failure is the end of the world. Failure should be a challenge.
If you don't get knocked on your ass ten or fifteen times in your life,
you'll never reach your level of excellence.
—Nick Bollettieri, Tennis Coach

My motivation is trying to prove everyone wrong who said I couldn't do it.
I've been that way my whole life, but failure's my biggest fear.
—Zach Thomas, Pro Bowl linebacker

Everyone has some fear. The man who has no fear belongs in a mental institution,
or on special teams.
—Walt Michaels, Football Coach

Even after an athlete minimizes the effect of external pressures by maintaining a healthy acceptance of responsibility and perspective, plenty of situations may still arise in which she might put pressure on herself. The next play may not be a life-or-death situation, but winning sure beats losing. A label for this feeling is the "fear of failure." It is normal and should be embraced, not denied. When it is real, but denied, it will still exist; however, the opportunity to deal with it effectively is gone. At some level, every person on the planet has a feeling of, "Oh no, what if I'm not good enough."

Having the strength of will to do what is difficult when acting scared would be easier takes many forms. Some are obvious, like staying down on a hard hit ground ball, trying a new task, or taking the stage in front of a large audience. Some are less obvious, like acknowledging a flawed belief, initiating an interpersonal conflict, or eating vegetables instead of cookies. A leader recognizes that everyone, starting with herself, has both flaws and the personal power to turn those flaws into strengths. Therefore, she embraces opportunities to get outside of her familiar/comfort zone and appreciates sources of information that clarify what is real and what is unreal for her.

Leaders embrace fear because it motivates them to work hard to avoid what it is they are scared of. Yes, fear is good! It is also bad when it causes the athlete to act scared, but such an effect is unnecessary. Leaders act courageously in the face of their fears. The important question is not "Are you scared?" It is "How do you behave when you are scared?" The leader's answer: "I will give my best effort one step at a time." She knows she is always good enough to do that!

Figure 19-2

Great Expectations

> Everyone pulls for David; nobody roots for Goliath.
> —Wilt Chamberlain, Basketball Hall of Famer

High expectations are an intriguing form of external pressure. The weight of expectations often proves to be more pressure than an athlete knows how to cope with effectively. She fails to find her trust mode "green" light because of things others are saying. Her desire to not let other people down gets in her way. She needs to remember that the most important person to please is herself. Examples of athletes who need to deal with high expectations effectively include high school athletes coming off a great game or season, players who are placed in an important role like pitcher or starter, and professional athletes who want to justify a large contract.

The "sophomore slump" typically results from failing to deal with expectations effectively. It manifests in many ways, but the root of the problem is that the first-year athlete was playing freely and enthusiastically. That attitude is lost in year two, replaced by fear/worry/pressure.

A better approach than trying to "make" it happen and live up to the expectations of others is to use all the available information to construct the best attitude for performance. High expectations can create some pressure, but if any athlete could choose between others expecting that she will do very well or very poorly, she would surely choose the high expectations every time. By controlling her attitude (which comes from the thoughts that she chooses to focus on), she can transform high expectations from a negative into a positive. It does not add pressure because she is already pressing herself to be the best she can be. It does add confidence because other people think she is skilled. This increase in confidence benefits her hype level, her attitude, and her focus. If she is smart, she also remembers to take nothing for granted and remain grateful for her opportunities.

Chapter 20

Do Your Job

> Don't tell me how rough the waters are. Just bring the ship in.
> —Chuck Knox, Football Coach
>
> A full mind is an empty bat.
> — Branch Rickey, Brooklyn Dodgers General Manager
>
> Thinking too much about how you're doing when you're doing it is disastrous.
> —Harvey Penick, Golf Instructor
>
> You have to be able to center yourself, to let all of your emotions go. Don't ever forget that you play with your soul as well as your body.
> —Kareem Abdul-Jabbar, Basketball Hall of Famer
>
> We compete, not so much against an opponent, but against ourselves. The real test is this: did I make my best effort on every play?
> —Bud Wilkinson, Football Coach

When it comes right down to an athletic performance, the goal is to keep it simple and think about nothing outside of the task at hand. Do the job by trusting it and letting it happen. This can be simplified to: do not think; just play. Simplify this to: focus. It is a bit ironic that mental skills training is about thinking effectively when its ultimate goal is to help athletes clear their minds. This skill is challenging, but it is also controllable. Leaders make practicing an ideal focus on the task at hand a priority and their skill improves accordingly.

Athletes are people, and people think, whether they want to or not. These thoughts affect performance, whether there is awareness or not. This is analogous to gravity. Gravity's impact is significant whether it is understood or not. The question for an athlete is not, "Do you think enough or too much?" It is, "Do you know when to think about what?" If you ask an athlete who was just in the zone what she was thinking about, more often than not, she will reply "nothing." Of course, if you ask her if she saw the ball (or another appropriate cue), the answer will be "very well!" This competitor was undistracted by other thoughts. She was focused.

Thinking too much can debilitate an athlete. Saying "don't think too much" almost never works. Not only is it negatively worded, but it also indicates an inappropriate focus on thinking rather than the task at hand. It is the opposite of trusting. Since an athlete's goal is to have a clear mind when she gets to that moment of truth, inappropriate thoughts should be consciously replaced. Lousy thoughts will happen, but that is not a significant problem. The athlete who allows herself to indulge in staying with the poor thoughts is the one with a problem. Awareness makes the adjustment possible.

The gathering process for changing poor self-talk into an appropriate focus can be as simple as a deep breath and a reminder of what is next. It can include an anchor, an image, a power phrase, or even a joke[22]. Gathering should be concluded with some sort of reminder to focus on what is next. If an athlete does not know where to start, she might try using a self-talk cue to, "Do my best at what I know." Or, "All I can do is all I can do."

Cathy Freeman, gold medal sprinter in the 2000 Olympics, said, "I was nervous, but I heard this voice in my head just telling me, 'Do what I know. Do what I know.' As long as I did that, I'd be fine." With practice, it becomes a leader's habit to focus narrowly on appropriate cues for the task at hand while thinking about "nothing."

Balance is everything. Following are some challenges to a leader's balance:

- Care, but do not try too hard!
- Make adjustments, but do not think too much.
- Always strive to improve, but do not dwell on mistakes.
- Similarly, try to be perfect, but do not ever expect it.
- Maintain high confidence without feeling satisfied and acting complacent.
- Be super-confident, but not cocky.
- Hustle and be quick, but do not hurry.
- Be enthusiastic, but not overexcited or nervous.
- Be a team player, but play for yourself first and foremost.
- Always be aggressive, but do not force it or try to make it happen.
- Be humble, but not deferent.
- Strive to be the best you can be while avoiding comparisons to others.
- Give yourself the best chance possible to get positive outcomes, but do not worry about things outside of your control.

---

[22] Jokes are great pattern interrupts during times of struggle. Did you hear what the guy said when he walked into a bar?............................"Ouch!"

PART 5:

NOW WHAT?

Experience by itself will not make you better. It is what you do with the experiences you have that matters.

Adversity can be a great motivator. Football, like anything else, is always a series of problems. Your success will depend on how well you are prepared and how well you handle those problems as they come along.
—Bill Walsh, Football Coach

Controllable behavior includes an athlete's approach, her performance, and her response. Approach, perform, and respond. It is a performance cycle that she will repeat over and over, with attitude having its major impact throughout. Each response morphs into the approach for what is next, so much of the mental skills of effective responses has been discussed above. Still ahead, chapter 21 discusses how to best respond to common on-field challenges. Chapter 22 discusses how to respond to life's greatest desires, using everything learned to set, pursue, and achieve effective goals. Chapter 23 takes it to the next level by tapping into the power of the group with a "T.E.A.M. First" mentality.

Leaders never stop learning and adjusting their thoughts and behaviors. They are responding to people and situations all the time. Their ability to connect with teammates provides both parties with resources that they would not have alone. Leaders make their teammates better by inspiring confidence in each step of the process of success.

CHAPTER 21

ACCELERATING PROGRESS

I found that if you are going to win games, you had better be ready to adapt.
—Scotty Bowman, Hockey Coach

If I make a mistake, I'm going to make a mistake aggressively and I'm going to make it quickly. I don't believe in sleeping on a decision.
—Bo Schembechler, Football Coach

Making appropriate adjustments is a critical aspect of behavior. No one is perfect and no athlete-as-scientist is successful (doing her best) unless her experiments are helping her move forward... fast. Athletes who learn faster will win more as they progress in the game. Leaders consistently coach themselves to repeat things they do effectively and change things that they could do better. This may be simple at times, but it is quite challenging at others. Unlike the laboratory scientist who controls for all but the experimental variable, the athlete has many factors affecting results[23] at once. Therefore, she must be able to glean information from patterns, not just what worked or did not work one time. Many athletes who are hoping to find an easy means to a difficult end (being a champion) demonstrate an unwillingness to analyze and adjust. Looking or hoping for an easy way out is immature; there are no shortcuts to success. Responding effectively is where leaders get an edge, because if accelerating progress was easy, everyone would do it!

Bridging the gap between potential and performance requires courage, honesty, and intelligence. Leaders are fine with learning that their former beliefs are not accurate. They are smart in part because they know what they do not know, and they know that intelligent people have simply become skilled at guessing. Others (e.g., coaches, teammates, and parents) may aid in the search for what works and how to do it, but it is ultimately each athlete's responsibility to find a way to get the job done. Leaders never stop learning, and they do what is right, even when it

---

[23] Reminder of terminological detail: *results* are completely controllable. *Outcomes* refer to what happens after the result.

means hurting now to help them reach their goals later. In fact, they recognize parallels between weight training and life: more pain usually means more gain. The best leaders even learn to like the right kinds of pain.

An athlete's discipline will allow her to successfully handle adversity. Andrew Carnegie said, "Disappointment and failure are two of the surest stepping stones to success." Said another way, the thinking pattern of champions is not that an event is bad or good. Rather, it is bad *and* good. Leaders seek to benefit from all situations and recognize that setbacks provide ripe information for figuring out what to adjust. If a game exposes a weakness, this is good news because it tells a competitor what to spend extra time working on. Leaders develop success from "failure."

An athlete's and a team's character is not revealed when everything is going well. It is revealed when adversity strikes. Everyone has adversity in their life and each occurrence provides an opportunity to practice managing emotions and move forward rather than backwards. "Flushing it" is a skill that should be practiced. Fortunately, there are plenty of chances to practice this on a softball diamond… and off.

The Ultimate Formula for Dealing with Adversity Successfully

1) Learn from it (whenever possible, or be patient and faithful to learn later).

2) Flush it.

Michael Jordan commented on this subject when he recalled that 26 times in his professional career he had been entrusted by his teammates to take the last second shot with a chance to tie or win the game and he missed. "Because of that," he said, "I succeeded." He was not great in spite of these "failures," but because of them. He knew that his misses were necessary to make him the player that he became. They taught him about some things that did not work, and he adjusted. They also taught him that he might miss the next one, but he was still the right person to have the ball in his hands with the clock winding down. Sometimes, the outcome would be good and sometimes it would be bad, but he knew how to give his team his best effort. Because of that, his chances at good outcomes were maximized.

Figure 21-1

A leader is relentless in the pursuit of her goal, which is to give her best effort one pitch at a time. She does not particularly need to be aware of how to do that when things are going well because she can just keep doing what she is doing. Awareness of what it takes to give her best effort is only needed when something needs to change. The steps of a best effort performance are a guide to finding the correct adjustment: create an ideal state[24], commit to a plan, and focus. Because of her knowledge of self and the game, she makes quick, subtle adjustments to maintain or regain balance. If she swings slightly under the ball, she knows it and how to adjust. If she is over-aggressive, same thing. Her relentless pursuit is the ability to quickly execute the never-ending need for subtle adjustments.

Ordinary behavior dictates that people usually wait for a mistake to occur before looking to make an adjustment. This is appropriate, but there are also times when a leader will recognize that a mistake is about to happen and adjust before it does. Typically, the pattern of mistake occurs over and over, eventually causing awareness. She has a natural tendency to rush, so she learns to remind herself in her pre-performance routine to slow down and let the game come to her. Inconsistent performers have to make a mistake many times before recognizing a need to adjust. Leaders notice quicker, sometimes to the point of making a pre-emptive adjustment before the mistake even happens.

---

[24] Motivation is part of an ideal state, but it might be worth listing as a separate step here. It should not be taken for granted; if the athlete does not care, she has no chance to give her best effort.

Awareness is key. Awareness is a synonym for truth, a recognition of the realities of the situation. The traffic light indicators[25] demonstrate awareness of key reference points. Aware athletes sometimes put a check of their own traffic signals into their pre-performance routines. At other times, familiarity with their signals allows them to simply notice when they are getting off track. The three lists (green, red, and yellow) should include attitude variables indicated by self-talk phrases, physiological variables such as being relaxed and energized, and behavioral patterns. To develop these lists, leaders review them often, adding to and adjusting them as awareness of key or more subtle variables rises. Outcomes are fine additions to her list, too, but if she wants to succeed in making an adjustment before making the mistake, she must have specific indicators that can be checked or noticed before beginning the performance.

Use that Multi-Billion Neuron Brain

It's not the experiences themselves that matter.
It's what you do with the experiences you have.

In the middle of difficulty lies opportunity.
—Albert Einstein

If experience is simply what has happened, it would not be particularly important. Experiences are valuable because athletes can learn from them. The goal is to have effective responses that lead to a good approach the next time a similar situation arises. How? Most athletes respond appropriately some of the time, but leaders do it systematically. After any situation, the questions they ask are:

1. What was I trying to do?
2. How did it go?
3. Why?
4. What do I want to do the next time that I find myself in a similar situation?
5. How might I achieve that?

Use of each of these questions after a performance is analogous to not skipping a step in solving a long division math problem. This ensures that the athlete/scientist attends to the appropriate details of the situation and forms hypotheses about how to improve the things that did not work.

---

[25] Appendix B – Traffic Light Analogy

The first question (What was I trying to do?) should have already been answered in the athlete's approach. Hopefully, she knew her specific and controllable job. The answer to the second question (How did it go?) should specifically address the first question, rather than falling into the pitfall of being outcome-oriented. If the performance went well, then the answer to the third question (Why?) is some version of "because I am skilled." Then, the answer to the fourth question (What do I want to do next time?) is "the same thing."

Figure 21-2

If the performance did not go as well as hoped, then the athlete will search for the reason. "I don't know" is the answer of most normal athletes. This makes sense because if she knew, she probably would have fixed it. But normal is not the goal; the "don't know" answer is easy… and unacceptable. She can guess. Some helpful guidelines for guessing follow.

Why did the performance not go well? First, a leader makes sure that it was her controllable behavior, not just the outcome, that was less than ideal. Next, she checks her focus. If she saw the play well, she checks hype level next. If she failed to focus appropriately or was out of control, awareness is critical because without it, her analysis may lead her to change the wrong thing. If she is satisfied by her focus and self-control, she moves on to the many other possibilities of strategy or mechanics and forms a best guess. Being intelligent is being good at guessing and noticing the quality of each guess over time. Leaders, thinking like scientists, get better and better at guessing with practice.

A poor response following one play almost inevitably leads to a poor approach on the next play. The disappointed or frustrated athlete who fails to ask the questions of an effective rational response and incorporate her answers into an effective approach to the next play is not accepting responsibility for her behavior. She is not putting the needs of the team in front of her own needs to dramatize or succumb to her struggles. She forgets that it is supposed to be difficult.

Athletes will respond to adversity either emotionally or rationally. Leaders choose rationally, thus dramatically increasing their chances of creating an ideal state for the next play. To give their best effort, they either maintain an even keel throughout or completely release the past (often by forgiving because nobody is perfect) before beginning their routine for the next play.

Table 21-1: Examples of Effective Rational Responses

What was I trying to do?	Throw the pitch aggressively through the target.
How did it go?	It missed down the middle, leading to a double.
Why?	I did not finish the delivery.
What do I want to do next time?	Finish the delivery aggressively.

What was I trying to do?	Throw the pitch aggressively through the target.
How did it go?	It missed down the middle, leading to a double.
Why?	I did not finish the delivery.
What do I want to do next time?	Finish the delivery aggressively.

What was I trying to do?	Hit a line drive where it was pitched.
How did it go?	I grounded out to short on an outside slow curve.
Why?	I was early.
What do I want to do next time?	Be patient and let the ball travel.

The last question is, "How might I achieve that?" Once the goal for next time is clarified, an educated guess should naturally follow. Again, "I don't know" is unacceptable. The simplest guess is a great place to start. Leaders often hypothesize that a reminder of what is desired will produce that result. If that does not work, they get creative in figuring out ways to effectively communicate from mind to body.

Sorry is a No-No!

There is no doubt in my mind that there are many ways to be a winner, but there is only one way to be a loser, and that is to fail and not look beyond the failure.
—Kyle Rote, Jr., Soccer Hall of Famer

Athletes should not say "my bad" or "I'm sorry." Teammates should not even tap their chest to tell others that they accept responsibility for their mistake. In *Love Story*, the theme is "Love means never having to say you're sorry." There is no need to apologize for making a mistake because humans are imperfect and the love is of the whole person, not just the perfect part. A commitment to the team (or oneself) carries the same concept. All people have flaws so athletes do not need to apologize for being imperfect. If an infielder boots a grounder, her teammates already know that she wishes she had not made the error. They also know whose mistake it was. Restating the obvious does not help anyone.

Unfortunately, apologies often unintentionally make the situation worse. For one thing, they sometimes let a teammate who could have helped the situation off the hook. The main problem, though, is that an apology often interferes with an effective rational response. Instead of thinking "How can I avoid that mistake in the future," the apologist feels better by apologizing. She thinks she has shown maturity by accepting responsibility for the mistake. In reality, fixing the mistake whenever another opportunity presents itself would be the most mature response. Athletes who accept responsibility but do not apologize allow themselves to regret the mistake, thus staying motivating to do something about it. In their determination to not let it happen again, they search for the way to make an appropriate adjustment. They ask the questions of an effective rational response. The point: it is not about feeling better, it is about getting better!

The challenging balancing act is to feel bad about the mistake while not losing a positive attitude simply for being a flawed human. This challenge is met by remembering to strive for perfection but never expect it.

Exceptions to this rule of not apologizing, as to almost every rule, do exist. First, this concept assumes that the athletes care. If doubt about caring exists, then an apology can show that it does. Second, sometimes it is unclear to the other person who is at fault. If the first athlete knows herself to be the guilty (and only guilty) party, apologizing will clarify the situation. This allows the other person to know that she does not need to make any adjustment. Third, an apology can prevent the other teammates' confidence from taking a blow, which is a method of protecting a teammate's fragile confidence. If the teammate is tough enough, she will not need to be protected in this way. If all members of a team are leaders who accept responsibility for doing their jobs and they are mentally tough, the desire to apologize will fade out. Focus will stay right where it should be: on getting the job done on the most important play in the game—the next one.

The Snowball of Destruction

The first rule of holes: when you find yourself in a hole, stop digging.

All of us do well when things are going well, but the thing that distinguishes athletes is the ability to do well in times of great stress, urgency, and pressure.
—Roger Staubach, Football Hall of Famer

Learn not to be careful.
—Diane Arbus, Photographer

People fall down. Winners get up. Gold medal winners get up the fastest.
—Bonnie St. John, Olympic Skier, Rhodes Scholar, and Amputee

Snowball effects, whereby a good performance leads to more good performances or a poor one leads to more poor ones, happen regularly to teams and to individuals. If momentum starts rolling in the good direction, let it roll. (Do not try to make momentum happen, just let it happen by continuing to do things right.) The negative snowball effect, unfortunately, is even more common and must be fought. One mistake will cause another only if it is allowed to.

The negative snowball effect happens because of a lack of emotional control, presentness, or confidence. A leader does not lose her confidence over a single mistake, a couple of single mistakes, or even a few. She knows it is completely within her control to keep her poise and her focus on the task at hand. She blocks the negative snowball effect largely by closely correlating her judgment about the quality of her performance with her level of focus and self-control.

No one plays perfectly all the time, but champions find a way to maintain an even keel, maintain or raise their confidence, and compete relentlessly. Leaders give a consistently superb effort. No matter what happens, they continue to create an effective performance state, commit to a plan of attack, and focus on the task at hand. They simply do not compound their mistakes. They are too mentally tough.

Leaders learn from experiences, then release them from consciousness. The event has served its purpose, so they flush it. All it can do now is damage. Unfortunately, thoughts about past performances often do this damage by initiating an emotional reaction. Negative emotions such as frustration, anger, impatience, and discouragement get in the way of logic. They also tend to linger, thus inhibiting future positive approaches. This behavior is normal; a leader's behavior includes awareness and emotional control plus the habit of maintaining positivism and enthusiasm through adversity.

This formula for success is, unfortunately, in direct contrast with human nature. Athletes (who are not thinking like scientists) get emotional about bad things happening, thus starting the negative snowball effect.

It is possible in softball to have a brief emotional response in some situations and not have behavior suffer. Brevity is key, because an effective rational response before the next play is needed. If the emotional response does not have a quick, definitive end, it almost always interferes with the implementation of an appropriate adjustment. Once it does end, both attitude and physiology need to return to the right place before the next play. Also, the brief emotional response should not be a damaging or embarrassing act in itself. For example, punching a bench and risking a broken hand is a bad idea, as is cursing in front of spectators. Instead, an athlete can squeeze grass inside a tight fist, then toss it away after something goes wrong. This is an appropriate and effective cue for her to use to release the past. It will work more often if forgiveness happens before the grass is tossed, and if it is practiced.

Learning not to have an emotional response to negative outcomes may be easier than learning how to have them and not let them interfere. It is certainly less risky. Many coaches make not acting out a rule. No throwing helmets. The point of this rule is *not* to encourage an emotional person to bottle it all up inside. Unfortunately, this is often the effect, so the negative snowball rolls on. The point of poise is to encourage the athlete to use her brain instead of reacting emotionally. Poor behavior (e.g., embarrassing or damaging outbursts and no adjustments) is a common result of poor or no use of the brain. Without analysis, no adjustment can be made. When an athlete learns to embrace challenges and even adversity, the outward demonstration of poise occurs more naturally. When she also appreciates the impact that body language has on her ability to create an ideal performance state, she will practice maintaining her internal and external poise until this literally becomes second nature.

Body language is a great indicator of emotional control. Posture and movements reflect attitude. An athlete can increase her awareness by observing her own unspoken communication. Then, with awareness, she can adjust before anyone else notices or before her less-than-ideal internal state affects her next play. If she does not adjust, she will communicate the wrong messages to herself, her teammates, her coaches, and even her opponents (building their confidence when they see her struggling. Some third base coaches have been known to watch the physical reaction of infielders in certain bunt or steal situations and call the next play accordingly).

Sometimes, an athlete has no idea of the negative vibes she sends off with her body language during practice or in competition. Since she lacks awareness, a pattern of behavior evolves. Watching a videotape of a recent example of this immature behavior can be an enlightening experience for this person.

Figure 21-3: Who can walk on water?

Over-analyzing is also a common mistake. Focusing on outcomes rather than behavior can lead to a search for adjustments when none is needed. For example, a hitter could inappropriately answer the question, "What am I trying to do?" with, "Get a base hit." She might behave ideally by swinging at a good pitch to hit and lining out to center field (process = good). Having a plan of attack that was outside of her control can lead this hitter to think that something went wrong in her performance. Therefore, she searches for an adjustment, believing incorrectly that she should not approach the next at-bat in the same manner as the last one.

Humans are not perfect. Therefore, in performance of any skill that gets repeated like pitching or hitting, not every attempt will come out just right. If things are going well but then one repetition is flawed, the athlete should not panic. The outlier should usually be written off as a one-time thing, keeping confidence high by assuming that the next one will be great again without any adjustment being made. Many athletes over-adjust because of the perfectionist's idea that every repetition should be flawless. Said a different way, athletes should not talk themselves into seeing a "yellow light" or "red light" when the light is actually "green."

Many softball teams have a player or two who can be seen rehearsing correct mechanics after nearly every flawed performance. The personality trait that leads to this often leads to paralysis by analysis as well. It is great to try to be perfect, but once a best guess is made about a needed adjustment, let it go. If the mistake has a decent chance of being a one-time thing, let it go. Often what is needed is trust, not to fix a mistake. Leaders recognize this tendency if they have it and discipline themselves to stop over-analyzing.

Figure 21-4

Athletes who change their behavior inappropriately in their search to solve a problem that may not exist can easily create a "slump." They make the wrong adjustments, digging themselves deeper into a hole. Using the questions of an effective rational response, starting with a specific and controllable goal, will significantly increase the likelihood of making only effective adjustments.

Sometimes, adjustments are motivated by others' behavior, which can be good or bad. If an athlete's approach gives her the best chance for success but the outcome did not work out in the short run, then she should stay with the approach. Perhaps her opponent simply had an exceptional performance of her own that time. Maybe it was just luck. She should be particularly hesitant to change anything if she has recently been "in the zone." A leader maintains that high confidence by letting a single poor outcome bounce quickly out of her consciousness. She might even tip her cap to her opponent, knowing that if she maintains her behavior, that other player may win an occasional battle, but she will not win the war.

The other possibility certainly exists—maybe the athlete should make a change. Patterns of poor outcomes can make it apparent that an athlete's approach is not giving her the best chance for positive outcomes. If luck seems to consistently be against her, perhaps it is not just chance that stinks, but her behavior. Honest judgment is required to help everyone learn her own tendencies. Statistics can aid this awareness development, as can asking the right questions. Does she tend to want to change too quickly or too slowly? Does she tend to go too fast or too slow in certain situations? Is she giving her best effort, or does she need to improve her preparation, her plan, or her focus? Leaders want to know.

Sometimes, a change is called for, but the athlete over-adjusts. Over-aggressiveness on one play leads to passiveness on the next. Trying too hard leads to a lack of intensity. Missing left leads to missing right. Being too early with the swing leads to being late. Taking a good pitch to hit leads to chasing a rise ball in the eyes. Furthermore, if rational thought does not identify this effect, the athlete becomes confused and frustrated. All sorts of things seem to be going wrong, and despite her efforts to use her brain to adjust, nothing seems to work.

Mistakes will happen, but a leader decreases the chances of having them happen to her. She trusts her preparation above all else. If she has prepared well and has experiences to use as reference points, she can better guess how far off track she is. Lack of preparation will cause an athlete to lack both confidence and skill in her approach and her responses. This obviously increases the chances of a "slump." The moral of the story: prepare, for there is no substitute for hard work.

What should an athlete do during competition when she has accurate awareness of a mechanical mistake and she wants to make an instant adjustment? She wants to fix the flaw, yet she does not want to have an inappropriate internal focus by thinking about it during the next play, either. A baserunner cannot think "keep my elbows in" and be completely focused on her job as she runs to second base. A hitter cannot think "hands inside the ball" and be completely focused on the ball. Both things can be thought about at the same time, but the athlete's focus would be distracted.

To solve this dilemma, an athlete must know how to get her mind and body to work together effectively. First, she should check her hype level. Often, physical mechanical mistakes are the result of the athlete's internal state. If self-control was not the issue, the solution is to image the mechanical correction during the approach to the next play. Then, she can move on to her trust mode for performing, confident that she has already made the appropriate adjustment. If her body has been trained with the muscle memory of correct mechanics and her hype level is under control, then this imaged reminder is all it will take to get her muscles to execute the skill correctly. Self-control and proper training are big "ifs," but they are controllable. To communicate effectively from mind to muscle, leaders imagine it first, then trust it and let it happen!

A final common mistake that causes the negative snowball effect is trying to "make up" for something that went wrong. Former NFL quarterback Browning Nagle said, "in certain situations we'd be down and the competitor in me would want to get it all back in one play. That impatience makes for bad plays and mistakes." If trying to "make up" for a mistake works, it shows that the original performance lacked intensity. If an athlete is unable to perform well until she has something to "make up" for, she should consciously "dial it up" *before* she makes the mistake.

If relentlessness already existed, this impatient attitude of "trying harder" will hurt performance because balance is lost. If she was already trying her hardest, how could trying harder help? Over-aggressiveness is assured. She should recognize that mistakes are inevitable. If she is giving her best effort for the good of the team and herself, neither apologizing nor "making up" for a mistake is necessary… or appropriate. Instead, she should simply continue to give her best effort one play at a time.

"Do your best" or "Do your job" every play, again and again. It is simple, but this leader's top priority is neither easy nor common. She controls her attitude and body, forms a controllable plan about what she wants to do, and then focuses and do it. Any athlete who succeeds in this daunting but controllable goal on each and every play on the diamond will be physically and mentally exhausted at the end of the game. She will also be pleased. Success is guaranteed if she agrees with Coach Wooden's definition: "success is the peace of mind that comes from knowing you did your best." What a great feeling to have earned that peace of mind!

Chapter 22

SMARTer Goals

The journey of a thousand miles begins with a single step.
-Lao-Tzu, Chinese Philosopher

*Whatever you can do, or dream you can, begin it.
Boldness has genius, power, and magic in it. Begin it now.*
—Johann Wolfgang von Goethe, Poet

Nothing is particularly hard if you divide it into small jobs.
—Henry Ford, Industrialist

*If you are bored with life, if you don't get up every morning with a burning desire
to do things, you don't have enough goals.*
—Lou Holtz, Football Coach

*The greatest danger for most of us is not that our aim is too high and we miss it,
but that it is too low and we reach it.*
—Michelangelo, Renaissance Artist

*Setting a goal is not the main thing. It is deciding how
you will go about achieving it and staying with that plan.*
—Tom Landry, Football Coach

The point of formal goals is to facilitate goal-directed behavior. That is, goals are useful because they help leaders direct attention appropriately, they provoke physical action on this focus, they improve time management skills, and they increase persistence (in large part by preventing frustration with the great distance of reaching long-term goals). Most elite athletes display goal-directed behavior much of the time. Still, actually writing goals down, then monitoring and adjusting them using specific guidelines can significantly increase and intensify this behavior.

Goals need to have certain characteristics and meet certain standards to be optimally effective. Diligently meeting these standards is an investment of time and effort; failing to do so can cause goals to hurt performance. Four Harvard

Business School professors produced a superb paper about the hazards of goal setting titled *Goals Gone Wild: The Systematic Side Effects of Over-Prescribing Goals*[26]. In it, they show that goals often have unintended side-effects that include a narrow focus that ignores non-goal areas, decreased intrinsic motivation, and distorted risk preferences. It is better to skip goal-setting than to do it without the guidelines below, especially including the follow-up monitoring and adjusting. Setting and maintaining optimally effective goals is uncommon. Discipline through the process will ensure that goals have the desired effects.

Written goals should be SMART+2—that is, they should be:

- **S**pecific
- **M**easurable
- **A**ttractive
- **R**ealistic
- **T**ime-Constrained

+

- Controllable
- Monitored and Adjusted

The SMART and controllable characteristics of optimally effective goals can and should be met with all daily or weekly goals. Goals for today or the near future can be completely controllable when they focus on the process rather than the product. Sometimes, new statistics must be invented to analyze completely controllable behavior. For example, a player may rate on a scale of 1-100 how focused she was on the task at hand today. The process of inventing and then keeping track of these new statistics is valuable for increasing awareness and making effective adjustments to relevant, controllable skills.

Once an athlete has selected her goals in measurable terms, she must find the right level to strive towards. The challenge is that it must always be both attractive and realistic. Unattractive goals do not motivate. Unrealistic goals also demotivate because they cause frustration.

Often it is impossible to definitively know that an attractive goal is realistic. A pursuit of the truth is required. Does she have a pretty clear picture about what it will take to reach that level, and is she willing to do all that work? If, after looking for and honestly evaluating all available information, a leader believes that she can achieve the goal, then it is acceptably

---

[26] http://www.hbs.edu/faculty/Publication%20Files/09-083.pdf

realistic. If she is honest and wrong, this is fine because all she can do is make her best guess now and the mistake will become apparent in the monitoring and adjusting process.

Leaders actively look for the appropriate level for each goal rather than simply guessing that what they want is realistic. They research available information by comparing their goal to their own past performances or other athletes' performances, and by listening to the opinions of coaches. They do not believe that something is unrealistic just because someone says it is. That could simply be a limiting belief. At the same time, they should not ignore evidence simply because it is not helpful for what they want.

The tendency among young Americans is to believe that they can do anything. While they do have unlimited potential, they also live in reality, not fantasyland. They may believe they can achieve extraordinary goals without extraordinary effort because they have not evaluated the available information or because they do not have awareness of how tough their goals actually are. Typically, they have not looked for this information because it is easier to do nothing than something, especially when the answers they find by doing something could be painful, scary, or intimidating. Leaders look, knowing the extraordinary achievement comes from extraordinary behavior.

Figure 22-1

If the athlete cannot find a level for a goal that is both realistic and attractive, then self-perceived "failure" is inevitable. She should reevaluate her set of beliefs (her perspective) so that success can be defined by something controllable. For example, many softball players would like to play professionally, but only a small minority will get the opportunity to do so. By no means does this mean that they cannot have wonderful experiences in softball. Dealing with this issue now is healthy and productive. Ignoring it does not cause the problem to go away. Balance is paramount, of course. No one knows the limits of an athlete's potential so a leader is realistic without ever selling herself short. The easiest way to do this is to focus on short-term goals and trust that the long-term will work out well if behavior is consistently good. The long-term goals serve as important "emotional buzz" generators. However, the key goals for driving specific behaviors are the short-termed ones.

Setting goals that are 100 percent SMART and controllable can limit the options, so the SMART+2 goal setting process is flexible. It is more important for short-term goals to be SMART and controllable than long-term goals. As the time constraint of long-term goals mutates them into short-term goals, the goals can be adjusted so that they come closer to meeting all six characteristics.

Some people would argue that a statistical goal such as wins in a season is inappropriate because it is dependent on many factors outside of the singular athlete's control. This issue is appropriate to consider, but if this statistic provides her a strong emotional "buzz," it should be kept. It will motivate her pursuit of effective short-term goals. "What do I need to do today to maximize my chances of achieving my long-term goals?" A leader knows that if she does not skip any steps and she still does not reach the goal for wins, she has not "failed."

The follow-up part of goal setting is critical, and it is the easiest place to get an edge over the competition. Effective goals must be monitored often and adjusted. Leaders work towards their season and lifetime goals every day using short-term (daily and weekly) goals. The monitoring process will prevent the goal from being forgotten or disregarded (e.g., New Year's resolutions). Such behavior would be damaging to self-esteem. Goals maintain their value only when they are regularly adjusted because this keeps them both attractive and realistic. When the athlete starts this process, finding the appropriate level for each goal is a "best guess" procedure. The quantity and quality of information available to make that guess increases dramatically with experience.

If the goal is no longer important, it should be dropped. If it becomes apparent that another variable is critical to reaching long-term goals, then a new goal should be added. The behavior of monitoring and adjusting goals takes discipline and is a clear mark of a champion.

Appendix J is a form for leaders to use in the pursuit of their goals. Appendices K and L make monitoring their daily and weekly goals precise and efficient.

Chapter 23

T.E.A.M. First

Together Everyone Accomplishes More

To achieve potential, the team must be greater than the sum of its parts.

Ubuntu: I am what I am because of who we all are.

Talent wins games, but teamwork and intelligence win championships.
—Michael Jordan, Basketball Hall of Famer

Teamwork is the beauty of sports. You become selfless.
—Mike Krzyzewski, Basketball Coach

The strength of the team is each individual member. The strength of each member is the team.
—Phil Jackson, Basketball Coach

For an individual to fully tap into her personal power, she needs support from others. It is the way humans operate. Positive energy is more than an idea. Proving the mechanisms for this to academic standards is difficult, but the results are inarguable. What works? Teams (sports, business, familial, or any teams) full of mutual respect for one another and teams with a culture of excellence, enthusiasm, and forgiveness work. Teams with great chemistry work.

Leaders in every industry want to put their finger on how to build chemistry. The answer is analogous to pursuing a peak performance - there is nothing that can guarantee it will happen, but it is appropriate to pursue anyway. By following certain principles, chances are maximized. This starts with a shared goal: team members have to care about the welfare of the team as a whole. If winning is not a universal priority, problems arise.

This book promotes the philosophy that "doing your best," in and of itself, defines success. It is important to notice that being successful maximizes the chances at winning. Leaders do their best to get better, faster, to promote winning. They also want to see their teammates get better, faster, to promote winning. They do not carry any resentment for the progress of teammates. They pursue, support, and celebrate learning. They also want to be healthy, stay out of trouble off the field, be in good standing in the classroom, and be part of a team that others would want to join. They want these things in large part because they promote winning.

Leaders not only have a vision of the goal of winning, they also have ideas about how to achieve this goal. They do not know the future, so specifics will vary, but they know that industriousness, positive energy, teamwork, and consistency are fundamental building blocks of success. They are like a rock; they do not get blown over by the shifting winds of circumstance. Their core beliefs about what is right are constant.

The next step for a leader to build chemistry is connecting with teammates. Teammates do not have to all like each other. Respect, however, is paramount. Respect requires acknowledging the other person's value; leaders make each team member feel important. They do not put themselves on a pedestal. Every member has an important role in making the team better, and their success is something the leader needs to help her reach her goals. For example, the last players on the bench are needed both to make teammates better and to be ready to perform when they get an opportunity.

Leaders communicate their appreciation of other people's value in many subtle ways every day. They smile, celebrate successes, notice otherwise unsung contributions, and share struggles. Because their appreciation for teammates is sincere, they will not be betrayed in a moment of weakness. This is important since respect is gained slowly, but can be lost very quickly.

Many people lose respect for one another when they disagree. This is avoided by remembering that either party could be wrong or partially wrong. If the other person is in fact wrong, forgiveness is the appropriate response. "Let he who is without sin cast the first stone," leaders recall. They realize that the past had to happen exactly as it did. Had they experienced the same things in life as another person, they are just as likely to be behind where that person is as ahead of it. However, the future is unwritten, so they hope and work for perfection in others (without expecting it), just as they do for themselves.

When respect is present, the critical pursuit of empathy naturally follows. Empathy is the ability to understand and be sensitive to the thoughts, attitudes, feelings, desires, and actions of another person. It is a skill like any other: some people are naturally better at it than others, but all people improve their skill with quality practice.

Babies are incapable of empathy. They are only able to think about what they want, not the motivations of others. People with Attention Deficit Disorder have a disadvantage for learning empathy. It is difficult for them to think about both what they want and another person's point of view at the same time. Empathy is a challenging skill for everyone. It is impossible to see the world exactly as someone else sees it because everyone brings a unique set of experiences and DNA[27] with them to the present moment. But leaders get closer.

The simplest way to practice empathy is to listen. Listening and hearing are different. Listening requires attention to what is being said. Leaders care about the welfare of others and they also have the confidence necessary to let go of their current desires. They know that if these released desires are important enough, they will have no trouble retrieving them from memory later. This allows them to focus on the task at hand: listening. Just as a hitter sees the ball big by being undistracted from the task at hand, effective listeners have a singular focus – figuring out what the speaker is trying to communicate.

Figure 23-1

Another component for developing empathy is curiosity. Being empathic is relatively easy when two people's motivations are similar. It is when there is disagreement that curiosity becomes critical. Rather than judging others, leaders are curious why someone would hold a different opinion or point of view. Curiosity leads to questions and questions lead to answers. Leaders connect because they are focused listeners and because they ask the right questions to figure out what the speaker is attempting to communicate. Doing (or saying) nothing is easier than doing something. Superb leaders are rare because they are not interested in what is easier, just what is better.

---

[27] The author is the proud father of identical twins. Even these girls are very different in the way they view the world.

But how can a leader respect a teammate who does something contrary to her core values? Perhaps the leader values hard work and the offensive behavior occurs when a hitter does not run out a pop-up. The assumption is that the batter does not care about the team. She is too selfish to hustle. Curiosity leads to a different conclusion: the lack of hustle likely comes from the precise opposite of not caring enough. It is caring too much. The pop-up disgusted the hitter so much that she had an emotional reaction that led her to forget to do her current job of sprinting to second base. Is this selfish behavior? Yes. Is it laziness? Yes, but not at its source. Armed with empathy, the leader is able to connect with this teammate, maximizing her chances of helping.

Figure 23-2

Often, mistakes are clear, but their sources are complex and hidden, even to the offending party[28]. In his classic book, *The Mental ABC's of Pitching*, Harvey Dorfman tells the story of a young professional pitcher who came into a minor league championship playoff game in the ninth inning of a tie game with a runner on second base and two outs. The first two pitches were strikes, but the next two were wild pitches that allowed the winning run to score. Afterwards, Harvey asked him what happened. The college graduate did not want to make excuses for himself, but he finally revealed that his college coach had a rule against giving up hits on 0-2 and 1-2 counts. The rule was this: allowing a hit means the pitcher will run "until he dropped." Dorfman: "Psychology 101: stimulus-response; conditioned reflex." All the pitcher thought about in those counts was, "Don't throw it anywhere close to the strike zone."

---

[28] In fact, if the mistake continues as a pattern, it is quite likely the person making the mistakes is unaware of the source. If she had awareness, an adjustment would then become possible.

Form Follows Function... or Dysfunction

> The time to make friends is before you need them.
> —John Wooden

> Great teams do not hold back with one another. They are unafraid to air their dirty laundry. They admit their mistakes, their weaknesses, and their concerns without fear of reprisal.
> —Patrick Lencioni, Author

> Show class, have pride, and display character. If you do, winning takes care of itself.
> —Paul "Bear" Bryant, Football Coach

Patrick Lencioni wrote a fable describing (and titled) *The Five Dysfunctions of a Team*. Those dysfunctions are absence of trust, fear of conflict, lack of commitment, avoidance of accountability, and inattention to results. All five are common within any team because people have a need for invulnerability. It is human nature to fear failure. Leaders overcome the dysfunctions by having the courage to battle them at each level. They trust their teammates and do not expect perfection. They are willing to expose their own vulnerabilities first, making it easier for their teammates to also do so. They mine for conflict rather than avoiding the discomfort it brings. They force clarity and closure by seeking answers and being willing to guess which course of action is best. Their accountability causes them to confront difficult issues head on, even learning to appreciate the pain of progress. Finally, leaders focus on collective results like the score of the games, not individual statistics like earned run average or batting average.

Communication is key. Communication is not defined by what the speaker intends to say. Rather, it is defined by what the other person or people understand. When there is agreement, meaning that the conveyed information matches the intended information, progress occurs. Reaching this agreement is largely the responsibility of the speaker. A simple and effective way to ensure agreement is for the speaker to ask the listener what she heard. Another strategy is to interpret body language. Speaker beware: some people nod in agreement out of habit, even when they do not fully understand what was said.[29]

Most communication is non-verbal. In a study of likes and dislikes, Albert Mehrabian, a psychology professor at UCLA, showed that 7% of communication came from words, 38% came from the way the words were said, and 55% of

---

[29] If this sentence caused you to wonder if you might nod without fully understanding, remember that awareness empowers effective adjustments.

transferred meaning came from non-verbal communications. Body language is a powerful source of information, both in communicating to self and to others. Attitudes are contagious; a teammate in a bad mood may say nothing, but she communicates plenty. Because of this, no team member will ever have a zero effect on the team. Each person is either a leader helping others move forward, or a drain on the chemistry and performance of the team.

Leaders attempt to nip problems in the bud. Sometimes, they recognize a poor behavioral pattern and try to help by addressing the problem non-confrontationally to the entire team. Sometimes, they engage in what they hope will be a productive feedback at an appropriate time and in a respectful way specifically with the offending party. For example, when a player is upset after making a mistake, a leader will often try to "pick her up." It may not work. Instead of appreciating the accurate, constructive feedback or support, the offending player snaps back or goes deeper into her shell. The leader must remember that she can only control her own behavior. All she can do is make her best guess about how to help. If the first attempt does not work, she can revise her strategy or increase her patience. Doing neither will pull her down with the teammate she is trying to help. Patience comes from remembering that any change by another person is outside of her control.

Leaders are not scared of engaging in productive conflict, but they are keen on finding an appropriate time to do so. During the game is not one of these times: they do not criticize teammates on the field or even in the dugout during games.[30] Rather, they look for opportunities to pick them up after a mistake. Sometimes they do this by saying something, but often they do it by making a play that minimizes the mistake. Instead of the pitcher thinking, "I should be out of this inning," she thinks, "That's okay. I will pick you up by getting ahead of this batter and getting her out." She knows that if she does not do her job, her teammate is likely to feel even worse about her mistake.

Leaders are on-field extensions of the coaching staff. They make sure that their teammates are in the right place and know what to do. If they sense that a teammate is not committed to her plan of attack, they stop the play before a problem occurs. Non-leaders do nothing, allowing the play to continue and hoping that the problem does not get exposed. They may even think to themselves that as long as it is someone else making the mistake and not them, the situation is acceptable. "Not my problem" is a common theme on teams with poor chemistry.

---

[30] This paragraph refers specifically to player-leaders, not coach-leaders. Coach-leaders, too, are wary of criticizing during games and do not allow themselves to do so out of frustration or anger. They may, however, correctly judge a criticism to be appropriate based on the circumstances.

Leaders Inspire Confidence

Leadership does not come from a title, it comes from skill. Leadership is the set of skills needed to make teammates better.

What you do makes a difference, and you have to decide
what kind of difference you want to make.
—Jane Goodall, Anthropologist and UN Messenger of Peace

When we love, we always strive to become better than we are. When we strive to become better than we are, everything around us becomes better, too.
—Paulo Coelho, Author

Perhaps the most important thing a leader does is what The Positive Coaching Alliance® calls filling teammates' emotional fuel tanks. With a full tank, people are more enthusiastic, confident, optimistic, coachable, and effective in dealing with adversity. With a full tank, they can go further. The first 22 chapters of this book focus on how to teach mental skills and how leaders fill that emotional tank for themselves, but humans are social beings. Most people gain or lose positive emotional fuel from the group more than from their self-coaching. Leaders get it. They are not only responsible for coaching themselves effectively to the best of their ability, but also others.

Since attitudes (including confidence) come from thoughts, leaders put useful thoughts into the brains of their teammates by saying them aloud. They fill their teammates' emotional fuel tanks with specific praise, appreciation, and positive non-verbal communications. Leaders do not hesitate to speak up. When the dugout is "dead," they cheer. When the pitcher is struggling, they have encouraging words to share. When practice is long, they are loud and proud, and they finish strong.

Some leaders are naturally vocal, but this is a struggle for others. It is important, though, so great leaders will find a way to give their teammates what they need. For example, a budding leader with a shy streak may use goal setting to hold herself accountable for speaking out once per game, inning, or batter. Or, she may be required to report one example of vocal leadership that was outside of her own comfort zone each day after practice to her coach.

Leaders particularly work to say what their teammates need when they recognize that a teammate's self-talk is counter-productive. For example, a perfectionist is likely to beat herself up over each mistake made in games, so the leader de-emphasizes the mistake for her by reminding her that it was just a one-time thing. Or, she tells her how great she was in the past, or will probably be again in the future. It is easier for the teammate to think confident and optimistic thoughts when she is hearing them from someone she respects.

Great leaders are rare. To become one, an otherwise normal person has set the example, tirelessly giving her best effort one step at a time. As if that is not enough, she also has to find the resources to support and challenge teammates. She helps focus the team on the task at hand, acts as a friend, counselor, liaison, and buffer, and solves problems. She is comfortable speaking with the coaches to express players' concerns. She even takes the initiative to organize events and situations to promote mutual respect, effective communication, and job clarity.

Leaders are most often found at the front of the pack. Conditioning drills are performed at an overall higher level when there is good leadership. For example, the coach may announce that the team will run ten 40-yard sprints. Most players will save some energy on the first few sprints so that they "have something left" on the last few. A leader knows that a sprint is defined by going all out, so she runs as fast as she can on the first one, not knowing how much energy she will have left in the tank later. However, she does know that she will deal with whatever pain comes later by doing her best one step at a time and accepting whatever happens. As promoted throughout this book, a leader brings the intensity of the "last one" to every repetition, and she does this whether anyone follows her lead or not.

Teamwork Rules

1. Every action and every inaction affects the team. The best way to improve the team is to improve yourself.
2. What your teammates really want from you is your best effort one play at a time -- no less is completely acceptable, and no more can ever be appropriately expected.
3. Anyone can do well when everything is going great. The measure of your character is how you respond to adversity.
4. Recognize the impact that all communication (verbal and non-verbal) has on others. "Winning" the mental game is contagious. So is losing.
5. It's human nature to indulge in negativity such as worries, thoughts related to "that's not fair," and many forms of "why doesn't my teammate play better?" Being normal does not excuse these selfish behaviors. Be unnatural: bring consistent positive energy to your teammates, showing your support particularly when they need it most - when they're struggling.

Leaders are not out front all of the time; great leaders also know when to follow. They recognize and support the good ideas of others. Sometimes, they do not know which direction to choose (nor are they expected to always know). When this happens, they are alert to see if anyone else has an idea of which path is best. If no one does and a guess is needed, they are willing to guess and be wrong. But if someone does have a good idea, they help draw it out of her. Leaders are honest about their insecurities, but consistently confident that they are giving their best effort and that this effort is what matters most.

Sometimes the hierarchy of a team dictates following. Freshmen, for example, should follow appropriate protocol to "earn their stripes." Carrying equipment or keeping charts is appropriate (though veteran *leaders* will assist with jobs like these). However, freshmen should oppose both hazing and suppression of their strengths. Hazing is the ignorant practice of rituals or other activities involving harassment, humiliation, or abuse used as a way of initiating a new player or players onto the team. When a hazing event is about to occur, a leader has the courage of her convictions to walk right up to the uninitiated and say, "I think this is stupid and you do not have to do it."

Suppression of strengths occurs when team veterans imply or state that a new player's opinions are not valid. Opinions are always valid, but they are not always useful, so a new player should be humble. She should be aware of her lack of experience competing at this level and respectful of those who have been there before. However, she should not hesitate to also be a vocal leader.

Another hierarchical time to follow is when a coach requires something and a leader has a different, better idea. This is typically a great time to stay quiet and follow. Differing opinions between a coach and a team leader can destroy the chemistry of the team. There are decisions that coaches must make, such as playing time and in-game strategies. If the coach chooses to ask players for input, fine. Otherwise, it is best for players to try not to have strong opinions about coaching decisions.

Coaches coach. Players play. Know the job and do the job. When players have strong opinions about coaching decisions, they risk that these will differ from the coach's opinions. If this happens, the player will lose positive energy. Even worse, if she shares this opinion with her teammates, she will sap their positive energy potential as well.

Many players do not realize that their opinions about coaching issues are a threat to the team's chemistry. Some who do realize this will have strong opinions anyways. It is in their nature. They can still lead effectively by "toting the party line" with teammates and discussing their opinions respectfully with coaches in private. Each minute of practice is valuable, so they would not want to sacrifice moving forward as a team, even for productive conflict. They express their views before or after practice.

Leaders either know their role, or they are on their way to figuring it out. This is easy on some teams and difficult on others. When it is tough, the leader uses her vision of what the team will look like as it succeeds to help her identify what questions to ask her teammates and coaches. She approaches each with respectful curiosity and leaves the potentially scary meeting with her leadership skills enhanced in multiple ways. Even when teammates[31] agree to disagree, respect and buy-in are enhanced. It is an absence of effective communication that typically saps these fundamentals of teamwork.

Leadership is never fake. Leaders do not pretend to be positive, they do not have to force themselves to care for others, and they do not need many pep talks to be motivated to compete. Faking can sometimes avoid problems for a day, but not for a season. The truth gets exposed. Leaders have a burning desire to win. They want to see teammates excel. They enjoy life, and especially softball. Their communications are consistently valuable because they are sincere.

Great leaders are not egoists who want to show off what they can do. Instead, they strive to, "let me show you what you can do." They believe that the world is full of opportunities worth working for and that since someone has to be on top, why not them? They are willing to do what is difficult, including striving for perfection one step at a time without ever expecting it, so why not indeed? Leaders inspire confidence in themselves and others by wanting success over comfort, by knowing what to do, and by doing what they know. And leaders inspire confidence because they do all this with relentless positivity.

---

[31] Coaches are teammates. They are not cohorts of players, obviously, but teammates are interdependent members of a team working towards common goals.

Five Leadership Lessons from Geese

Lesson 1 - Achieving Goals
Geese migrate thousands of miles each year. Speed is critical. The birds use a 'V' or 'U' formation to take advantage of a wing-tip vortex, reducing drag and saving as much as 50% energy.
The point: Together we can do more than we can do alone. Would you rather run three miles by yourself or with your teammates? You might be able to do it yourself, but it is easier with others.

Lesson 2 - Encouragement
Geese flying in formation 'HONK' to encourage those up front to keep their speed up.
The point: Encouraging teammates to do what needs to be done is not childish or superfluous. Some people need it more than others. If it works, do it, and avoid being too shy to find out if it works. Look for ways to empower each other. It is necessary to show extra support in trying times.

Lesson 3 - Stay Together
When a goose falls out of formation it suddenly feels the drag and resistance of flying alone. It quickly moves back to take advantage of the literally uplifting power of the birds in front.
The point: You need your teammates to achieve your personal potential and team victories. Stay in formation and appreciate the opportunity to both give and receive help.

Lesson 4 - Sharing
When a goose tires of flying up front it drops back into formation and another goose flies to the front.
The point: It makes sense to take turns doing the hard tasks. Respect and protect each other's unique arrangement of skills and resources. If something a teammate does bothers you, realize first that you have almost no clue what that person has been through in life. Whatever has led to here, your job now is not to criticize, but to support.

Lesson 5 - Empathy and Support
When a goose gets sick, two geese drop out of formation and follow it down to the ground to help and protect it.
The point: Stand by each other in difficult times. It is often difficult to do the right thing when the 'poop' is hitting the fan, but this is when you have the opportunity to define your character with courage and helpfulness!

IT ALL COMES DOWN TO ONE PITCH: PART 2

Man's finest hour is the moment when he has worked his heart out in a good cause and lies exhausted on the field of battle, victorious.
—Vince Lombardi, Football Coach

(Continued from Part 1 at the beginning of the book.)

Upon arriving at this point, your imagination is returned to Ashley and the ninth inning of a championship ballgame with the bases loaded and two outs. As stated, Ashley "must step into the batter's box" with the season hanging in the balance. A moment ago, she had a thought that this could be her final at-bat in softball at this level. Fortunately, Ashley's mental skills training helped her to quickly recognize this as a distraction, so she told herself, "Hey, keep it here. Do your job."

Ashley knows that her job includes creating a feeling of confidence. This is not difficult because she is thoroughly prepared, both physically and mentally, for this at-bat. Her on-deck routine only lasts the length of time of two pitches to the batter in front of her. If the at-bat only took one pitch, the game would have to wait a few seconds while she finished. If it took more, as this one had, she used the extra pitches to reaffirm the timing of her stride, matching it with the timing needed to hit this pitcher's fastest inside screwball. She also took a few more quality practice cuts.

Ashley's routine included putting on her warrior tools (helmet and batting gloves) just before she was in the hole. Next she stretched, specifically focusing on her back and shoulders. Then when on-deck, she took a few big arm swings with a bat to loosen her shoulders more, followed by three bottom-hand and three top-hand one-armed swings of the bat. Next, she took three full cuts, imaging a line drive with backspin into the right-center field gap coming effortlessly off her bat on each. She found this routine anchored her confidence better than others she had previously tried. Therefore, her confidence and superior self-talk allow her to think not that he "has to" hit now, but rather that he enthusiastically "gets to" hit with the game on the line. *What could be better?*

So now the big moment that Ashley worked so hard to prepare for has arrived. If she gets a hit to the outfield, her team will win, and she will be mauled near first base by 16 ecstatic teammates, forever labeled a hero. If she makes an out… she will be disappointed. However, Ashley, her coaches, and her parents know that she will be no better or worse of a person tomorrow than she is today, no matter what happens. They will be proud that she truly gave her best effort to the most "important" at-bat of her life, and she will have performed (behaved) admirably. This may or may not be enough for a victory in this game of softball, but it is certainly enough for a victory in the game of life. Win or lose, Ashley's opinion of herself will not change.

As she steps into the box, Ashley knows all this, deep down, but is not thinking about it at the moment. Instead, she is still going through the same routine she has performed, without exception, for the past 75 at-bats of this spring. She knows she is in control of herself, she has an aggressive plan of attack based on the situation, she is physically loose and has reinforced positive muscle memory, and she knows exactly where this pitcher's release point will be. Now as she crosses into the batter's box, she is anchoring her self-trust to perform aggressively by saying to herself, "I got this; hunt the ball" and patting her right hand on her right thigh.

As the pitcher agrees to the catcher's sign, Ashley's final pre-swing thought is simply, "See it and be easy." Then her mind is quiet. In a moment, her external focus will switch from 'broad' (the pitcher) to 'preparatory narrow' (the pitcher's right hip) to 'narrow' (the specific area where the ball will be released within the next few hundredths of a second). She will successfully see the ball at release and track it as it travels toward home plate at over 60 miles per hour. Well under a half of a second later, the ball will fly into the hitting zone in the same manner that Ashley imagined it would last night, in her hotel bed. She had imagined other situations also, but her teammates are glad she included this one: a first-pitch curveball on the outer third of the plate.

In sum, Ashley has succeeded in approaching her potential to perform at this exact moment in time. Wow! Without conscious thought and seemingly without any particular effort, she will uncoil and the bat head will explode into the hitting zone. And when the bat hits the ball, will Ashley get a base hit? Will Ashley be a hero?

I do not know.

And yes.

Appendix A – Reflective Worksheet

Learning is Most Important on _____
(today's date)

Today's activity was a:

    Team Practice   Game Day   Individual Workout

(Scale of 1-10)

____ How well did you maintain a positive ATTITUDE today?
____ How well did you maintain high CONFIDENCE today?
____ How well did you stay FOCUSED on the task-at-hand today?
____ How well did you TRUST your stuff, your plan, and your teammates today?
____ How HYPED were you today, on average?
____ How HYPED up would you *like* to have been today, on average?

Was there a situation today in which you could've given a better effort if you were more hyped up or more calm?

If so, how might you achieve that ideal state next time?

What are a couple things you did well that you want to remember to do in the future?

What skills or situations did you successfully identify as needing improvement?

Did you stop to gather yourself after any adversity today? If so, did it work?

If not and you wish you had, what cue will you use to help you remember to gather next time?

Appendix B - Traffic Light Analogy

Indicators for _____   _____
                               (Activity)   (Date first recorded)

RED

YELLOW

GREEN

Appendix C – The Eight Mental Skills of Great Athletes Awareness Exercise

Successful Athletes Excel in Eight Categories of Mental Skills

Instructions: Rate how skilled you believe you are right now at each specific skill by placing a number from 1-10 in each blank, 10 being the best possible score.

1. POSITIVE ATTITUDE

Successful athletes…
_____ Realize and agree that *choosing* a positive attitude is totally within their control.
_____ Realize and agree with Wooden's advice: "*Strive for perfection, but never expect it.*"
_____ *Learn* from both their successes and "failures."
_____ Stay positive through adversity, as long as they survive.
_____ Do not allow themselves to worry about things outside of their control.
_____ Maintain *balance* between sport and other aspects of their lives.

2. Self-Talk

Successful athletes…
_____ Are *aware* of the self-talk they have in training, before competition, and during competition. This is a tough question because you don't know what you don't know. Just take your best guess!
_____ Use self-talk to maintain their self-*confidence* at all times, even during or after adversity.
_____ Talk to themselves with **dignity** and **respect**, as if talking to a friend.
_____ Use self-talk to regulate their feelings and behaviors during competition.
_____ Quickly and effectively reframe or counter negative thoughts into positive ones.
_____ Consistently get to their own *TRUST MODE* when it is time to perform so that they do not think too much while performing.

3. Motivation

Successful athletes…
_____ Are *self-motivated* to achieve desired results and peak performances.
_____ Agree that motivation is a *skill* that should be *practiced*.
_____ Stoke their own fire *daily* as much as necessary to achieve consistently motivated behaviors.
_____ Are *persistent* through difficult tasks and difficult times.
_____ Appreciate that many of the most important benefits of sport come from participation in the *process* of playing the game, not from its outcomes.
_____ Are *relentless* in their pursuit of excellence.

4. Goals and Commitment

Successful athletes...
_____ *Set* long- and short-term *goals* that are specific, measurable, attractive, realistic, time-constrained, and controllable (SMART + 1).
_____ Are *committed* to attaining their goals, and...
_____ Understand that doing so requires that these goals are *monitored* and *adjusted regularly*.
_____ Write their goals down and keep up with them, adjusting them as needed to maintain a level for each short-term goal that is both attractive and realistic.

5. People Skills

Successful athletes have a healthy perspective on life and sport. They...
_____ Are not just willing, but actually *eager* to put the needs of the team in front of their personal desires.
_____ *Communicate* their thoughts, feelings, and needs to themselves and others appropriately.
_____ *Listen* to coaches, teammates, officials, families, and friends appropriately.
_____ Effectively deal with *conflict*, difficult opponents, and other people who are negative.

6. Concentration and Focus

Successful athletes *know their job* and *do their job*. That means, they...
_____ Know their sport well enough to know where to *direct* their *attention* according to the performance situation.
_____ Effectively maintain *concentration* and resist distractions.
_____ *Commit* to a plan-of-attack that is *aggressive under control* before engaging in the action.
_____ Are able to quickly and effectively *refocus* when concentration is lost during competition.
_____ Stay in the present moment by *avoiding potential distractions from the past*, such as mistakes by self, teammates, or umpires.
_____ Stay in the present moment by *avoiding potential distractions from the future*, such as winning or what others will think.

7. Self-Control

Successful athletes...
_____ Believe that their *best effort* is *always* good enough.
_____ Know *how* to be comfortable in situations that would make most people uncomfortable.

_____ *Recognize* that nervousness and excitement can help them perform well and achieve peak performance.
_____ *Know how* to reduce anxiety when it becomes too strong or inappropriate without losing intensity or focus.
_____ *Understand* that strong emotions such as excitement and disappointment are part of the sport experience.
_____ Are able to *regulate and channel emotions* to improve their performance, rather than interfere with it.

8. Imagery

Successful athletes…
_____ Practice *imagery*.
_____ *Have figured out* how to use this powerful tool to most effectively aid their own positive mind-body connection.
_____ Prepare themselves effectively *at practice* by imagining themselves performing well in competition.
_____ Create and use mental images that are personal, detailed, specific, and realistic.
_____ *Use* imagery in their Countdown to Competition (before the contest).
_____ *Use* imagery during the contest to effectively communicate mind-to-muscle.
_____ *Use* imagery after the contest to increase awareness and aid effective adjustments.

Appendix D – Leadership Evaluation with 360° Feedback

This leadership awareness exercise is designed to initiate thought about some leadership traits that you do well and some that you could do better. Score each concept on a scale of 1-100, with 100 as the best possible score. First, score where you think you are. Then if you choose to complete the 360° feedback, rate how you think others within your immediate team view you and get them to rate how they actually view you.

Vision

_____ a)   I have a clear conception of where we are going together.
_____ b)   I believe that success is a process not a destination. This belief is reflected by my actions.
_____ c)   I have the ability to communicate my vision to others.
_____ d)   I work hard.

People Skills / My Care for Others

_____ a)   I am visible and available / Openness for teammates about self
_____ b)   Listening skills
_____ c)   Trustworthy in the trenches
_____ d)   Building Relationships – I am good at following John Wooden's advice: "The time to make friends is before you need them."

Time Management Skills

_____ a)   I am on time or early for all of my appointments.
_____ b)   I make time for important projects that don't have to be completed today.
_____ c)   I make time to care for myself (e.g. eating healthy, sleeping enough, working out).

Character

_____ a)   Honesty and Integrity – I am honest, forthright, and my thoughts, words, and actions all jive comfortably with each other according to my values.
_____ b)   Humility – I respect every person, know that I am flawed, and steadily seek to improve myself.

_____ **Competence** – I am skilled and knowledgeable in my field.

Attitude
____ a) Lead with optimism, enthusiasm and positive energy, guard against pessimism and weed out negativity.
____ b) Consistently confident and avoid complaining.

Initiative and Boldness
____ a) I recognize budding problems and actively seek solutions.
____ b) I will not permit fear of failure or laziness to stop me from doing what I think is right.

____ **I Have a Serving Heart**

Appendix E – Values Exercise

VALUES
They're immeasurably valuable. Do you know yours?

Directions: First, read through the list of values and their definitions and circle the ones that are important to you. This is likely to be most of them. You may change a definition or add additional values if you like. Do not skip ahead at any time during this exercise.

FAITH
- Belief and Trust

HONESTY
- Telling the truth
- Does not engage in deception
- Is forthright and candid.

HARD WORK
- Mental and/or physical labor
- Energy and persistence

TRUST
- Belief and faith in someone's ability to do something.

TEAMWORK
- Working together to achieve results.

SKILLS
- Development of the ability to do something well… on command.

PROFESSIONALISM
- Demonstration of the highest level of skill and competence
- Acceptance of role
- Consistency

FUN
- Enjoyment of an activity.

DECISIVENESS
- The ability to make decisions firmly, clearly, conclusively, and in a timely manner.

RESPONSIBILITY
- Taking ownership for personal choices.
- Admitting mistakes and "failures."
- Taking accountability for someone or something

COMPASSION
- Active caring or concern for others.

LOYALTY
- Allegiances to people, organizations, ideals, causes, etc.

COMPETITION
- Comparison of self, team, or organization against oneself or another.

FOCUS
- Giving attention to the task at hand.

EXCELLENCE
- Pursuit of the highest level of performance.
- Doing common things in uncommon ways.

UNSELFISHNESS
- Placing more importance on others' needs than your own.

RELENTLESSNESS
- Unyielding, merciless
- Persistent without emotion

INTEGRITY
- Thoughts, words, and actions are all in alignment with each other.
- Standing up for what is right.
- Walking the talk.

DIVERSITY
- Appreciates and respects individual and group differences.

CONFIDENCE
- A solid belief in one's skills and abilities
- Can be situation specific or general

RESPECT
- To hold an individual's skills and abilities in high regard

MORAL COURAGE
- The strength of will to do what is emotionally difficult.
- Willing to risk ostracism, adversity, embarrassment

COMMITMENT
- A stated dedication to someone or something

PHYSICAL COURAGE
- The strength of will to do what is physically difficult
- Risking or enduring pain or injury

DISCIPLINE
- Holding oneself or a group to a high standard of behavior in a habitual way.

RESILIENCY
- The ability to bounce back from setbacks or unexpected results
- Getting back on a successful track

HELPING OTHERS
- Placing importance on assisting other people.

HEALTH
- Placing importance on physical and emotional well-being.
- The absence of disease.

POSITIVE ATTITUDE
- Expressing an upbeat, optimistic way of thinking, feeling, and acting
- No complaining
- No blaming

WINNING
- Scoring more than the opposition.
- It's better than the alternative.

TRADITION
- Respect for customs and beliefs.
- Doing things a certain way based on past experience.

MONEY
- Financial assets.
- The accumulation of wealth and possessions.

EDUCATION
- Placing importance on learning.

FAME
- Recognition by others.
- Desire to be well-known.

FORGIVENESS
- Letting go of one's own mistakes.
- Letting go of others' mistakes.

FRIENDSHIP
- Strong ties with family, friends, co-workers, teammates, or members of a certain community

PRIDE
- Values the efforts of self and others.
- Representing yourself and your team in a positive manner.

ACHIEVEMENT
- ➤ To reach or attain a desired goal or to complete a project successfully.

PATIENCE
- ➤ Accept or tolerate, delay gratification without getting upset or angry.

TOUGHNESS
- ➤ The ability to deal with hardship, overcome difficulty, and continue to be effective.

ENTHUSIASM
- ➤ Demonstrating a high level of energy and effort.

PLAY
- ➤ Imagination, spontaneity; the ability to be amused.
- ➤ Engagement/participation.

STATUS
- ➤ Placing importance on rank, position, or relative standing.

RELATIONSHIPS
- ➤ Connections between and among people.

FLEXIBILITY
- ➤ The ability to adapt to different environments, conditions, or change.

SPORTSMANSHIP
- ➤ Respect for self, others, and the game.

FAMILY
- ➤ Connection to immediate or extended relations.

LEADERSHIP
- ➤ The ability to create relationships in order to complete a stated goal.
- ➤ Being a role model and helping others to achieve, too.

CREATIVITY
- ➤ Placing importance on imagination, inspiration, and inventiveness.

MEANINGFUL WORK
- ➤ Doing and providing work that has a purpose and/or significance

CONSISTENCY
- ➤ Performing with little variation over time

Next, using the circled values above, trim your list to the 15 (or so) values you hold in the highest regard. Which ones are most important to you?

My top 15 (or so) values:

_____   _____   _____

_____   _____   _____

_____   _____   _____

_____   _____   _____

_____   _____   _____

Do not skip ahead at any point in this exercise. Now that you have your top 15 values, go through this new list and circle your top ten. There will be overlap and they are all important, but pick the ten that are most meaningful to you.

Finally, go through your top ten values and trim the list once more to your top five, write them below. Then live by them.

My top five values:

_____   _____

_____

_____   _____

Appendix F – Positive Emotional Flood Exercise

Sometimes positive energy is the solution. You might access this list when times are rough, or use it to create a buzz of enthusiasm and confidence before a "big" performance. The idea now is to make a written database of memories that you can access later, as needed. The process of remembering can be fun in itself. You've already experienced all the positive emotions that you'll seek in the future. Now, take your time (don't press) and let the memories flow. (It's not important to record details or private information. Simply record enough to remind yourself of the specific memory later.)

You are looking for a written record of times when you have felt joyful, love, humor, excited, pride and/or grateful. Also, which of your many achievements stand out as your best. After opening your mind with deep breathing, search your amazing database of memories for the top two to four actual examples of positive memories related to each:

When did you feel...

Joyful

1.

2.

3 (optional).

4 (optional).

Humor

1.

2.

3 (optional).

4 (optional).

Love (connected to another person)

1.

2.

3 (optional).

4 (optional).

Excited

1.

2.

3 (optional).

4 (optional).

Proud

1.

2.

3 (optional).

4 (optional).

Grateful

1.

2.

3 (optional).

4 (optional).

Achievements

1.

2.

3 (optional).

4 (optional).

Appendix G – Routines for a Specific Game Situation

Step	Reason

Appendix H – Pre-Game Routine

Step	Reason

Appendix I – Gathering Routine

Step	Reason

Appendix J – Stop the Day, Start the Game[32]

The key to being locked in and focused is to have a plan of how you will get your mind right, regardless of what occurs in your life and in your sport that day. Use this worksheet to design your own Mental Game Plan to practice and utilize specific tools in your mental skills toolbox.

1. First, control the controllables, meaning yourself. "Stop the day" by getting your consciousness rid of distractions from outside of softball. Inside the gate, you get a break from your problems, so park them outside just before you walk through the gate. You can come back to them up later.

How do *you* stop the day? (e.g. cell phone off; body inside the fences = mind inside the fences)

2. The next element is to set the intention for what you want to accomplish today. This is done by setting specific process goals and bringing as much of your ideal performance state (e.g. the energy, focus, and confidence) from your P.P.P.P. to today's practice or game as possible.

Write down a title for your P.P.P.P.

3. Define (perhaps written in a logbook) two specific goals for today and a hypothesis for each about how you will accomplish it. When you put on your cleats at the field, remind yourself of these two goals and when you take them off, evaluate how well you achieved them.

4. To transition effectively into softball, initially use the following protocol, then after you have some comfort with it, tweak it to fit your personal needs.
    a. Centering breaths (30 seconds)
    b. Attitude of Gratitude (45 seconds of appreciation for blessings in your life)
    c. Imagery: P.P.P.P. (60 seconds)

---

[32] Josh Lifrak, Mental Conditioning Coach at IMG Academies, contributed significantly to the design of this mental exercise.

- d. Imagery: Execution of fundamentals of your game (60 seconds)
- e. Imagery: Execution of achievement of your daily goals (60 seconds)
- f. Centering breaths (15-30 seconds)

Record when and where you will stop the day and start the game by going through your imagery/mental rehearsal.

5. Use power phrases to spark your mind while you play. Say each phrase 3 times during or at the conclusion of physical stretching or dynamic warm-ups. Then, use them as part of your pre-performance or gathering routines while you play. Tips for creating power phrases:
    a. Define an aspect of your game you are working on and state that this part is solidly an asset.
    b. Accentuate the strengths of your game (e.g. I run hard and fast. I outwork my opponents.)

Write down three power phrases now and add to the list as you find more that work well for you.

Appendix K - Goal Setting Worksheet #1

Instructions: Record as many goals as you want. Each one should be important to you. Check each goal against the box on the right to see if it is as *SMART* and *controllable* as you can make it. Take your time doing this, researching issues with coaches, friends, on the Internet, etc. When you finish, you should see some logic from the bottom to the top of the page. If you succeed in your daily and weekly completely controllable goals, it should logically follow that you will likely meet your single-game goals, which if achieved should allow you to meet your season's goals, which if achieved should allow you to meet your lifetime's goals (or mission). Record your long-term goals first, using the list from your Mission Exercise in Chapter 5 for ideas. Good luck! You can do it!

My Performance Specific Goals

By _____ Date first recorded:_____

My lifetime goals are to:

Specific
Measurable
Attractive
Realistic
Time Constrained
Controllable

My goals for the upcoming season are to:

In each performance, I would like and expect to achieve these goals:

Day to day or each week, my goals are to:

Appendix L – Short-Term Goal Tracking

Directions: Record each optimally worded goal below and the scale it will be judged on, whether that is 1-10, 1-100, Yes/No, time, or A/B/C/D/F. You may want to add a one-word reminder of each goal in the box at the top on the daily log. Monitor and adjust this list regularly (recommendation: biweekly)[33].

Record each daily and weekly goal, specifically	Scale it will be judged on
1.	
2.	
3.	
4.	
5.	
6.	

---

[33] Appendices J, K, and L are available free on regular sized paper by emailing "Goal worksheets, please" to the author at aaron@CoachTraub.com.

Appendix M – Daily and Weekly Goal Log

Date	Goal #1	Goal #2	Goal #3	Goal #4	Goal #5	Goal #6	Total Goals Met	Comments / Special Circumstances
Week:								
Week:								
Week:								
Week:								
Week:								
Week:								

Week:								
Week:								
Week:								
Week:								
Week:								
Week:								

References and Suggested Reading

Branden, Nathaniel (1994). *The Six Pillars of Self-Esteem*. New York: Bantam Books.

Branden, Nathaniel (2000). *The Art of Living Consciously*. New York: Bantam Books.

Biro, Brian (1997). *Beyond Success: The 15 Secrets of a Winning Life*. Asheville, NC: Pygmalion Press.

Carnegie, Dale (1936). *How to Win Friends and Influence People*. New York: Pocket Books.

Covey, Stephen R. (1989). *The Seven Habits of Highly Effective People*. New York: Simon and Schuster.

Dorfman, H.A. (2000). *The Mental ABC's of Pitching: A Handbook for Performance Enhancement*. South Bend, IN: Diamond Communications, Inc.

Dorfman, H.A. & Keuhl, K. (1989). *The Mental Game of Baseball: A Guide to Peak Performance*. South Bend, IN: Diamond Communications, Inc.

Frankl, Viktor E. (1959). Man's Search for Meaning. Boston, MA: Beacon Press.

Gallwey, Tim (1974). *The Inner Game of Tennis: The Classic Guide to the Mental Side of Peak Performance*. New York: Random House.

Gordon, Jon (2007). *The Energy Bus*. Hoboken, NJ: John Wiley & Sons, Inc.

Jeter, Derek (2000). *The Life You Imagine*. New York: Three Rivers Press.

Jordan, Michael (1998). *For the Love of the Game: My Story*. New York: Crown Publishers.

Kauss, David (2001). *Mastering Your Inner Game*. Champaign, IL: Human Kinetics.

Lencioni, Patrick (2002). *The Five Dysfunctions of a Team*. Jossey-Bass: San Francisco, CA.

Mack, Gary with Casstevens, David (2001). *Mind Gym: An Athlete's Guide to Inner Excellence*. New York: Contemporary Books.

Peck, M.S. (1978). *The Road Less Traveled: A New Psychology of Love, Traditional Values and Spiritual Growth.* New York: Phoenix Press.

Ravizza, K. & Hanson, T. (1995). *Heads-Up Baseball: Playing the Game One Pitch at a Time.* Indianapolis, IN: Masters Press.

Robbins, Anthony (1986). *Unlimited Power.* New York: Simon and Schuster.

Robbins, Anthony (1991). *Awaken the Giant Within.* New York: Simon and Schuster.

Don Miguel Ruiz (1997). *The Four Agreements: A Practice Guide to Personal Freedom.* San Rafael, CA: Amber-Allen Publishing, Inc.

Williams, J. (Editor), *Applied Sport Psychology: Personal Growth to Peak Performance.* Mountainview, CA: Mayfield.

Wooden, John (1997). *Wooden: A Lifetime of Observations and Reflections On and Off the Court.* Chicago, IL: Contemporary Books.

Suggested Audio Lessons: Coach Traub's Elite Athlete Audios

Crisp. Convenient. Inspirational.

A library of audio lessons for today's athletic leaders, Coach Traub's Elite Athlete Audios share the mental strategies of the greatest athletes in the world with you! Each audio lesson is under five minutes. Two are free here with your QR Code Reader: listen to each .mp3 file in your web browser. All are available on iTunes, Amazon, Facebook, and all normal music distribution sites.

EAA # 1 - Mental Toughness

EAA #3 - Confidence

Notes

About the Author

Aaron Weintraub is a coach, speaker, and consultant dedicated to helping athletes and coaches "win" the mental side of the game. After 13 years as a college baseball coach, Weintraub became a full-time mental skills coach in 2006. Since then, his clients have included Baylor University, University of Houston, Dallas Baptist University, University of Texas at Arlington, Blinn College, Georgia Tech, Michael Johnson Performance and many other teams and individuals. He speaks regularly at coaching conventions and workshops. In 2012, Weintraub began releasing Coach Traub's **Elite Athlete Audios, a library of crisp, convenient, and inspirational mental training lessons**. They are available on iTunes, Amazon, Facebook, and other .mp3 outlets.

Weintraub received a bachelor's degree in sociology from Emory University and a master's degree from the University of Virginia. At Virginia, he studied sport psychology and motor learning under Dr. Linda Bunker.

Weintraub coached college baseball from 1994 to 2006. In 2001, he helped lead the Emory University Eagles to their first ever #1 national ranking on the way to a final record of 36-9. From 2002 to 2006, Weintraub coached at Cedar Valley Junior College in Dallas. He helped the Suns grow from a 13-38 team to a well-respected, consistent winner. The team was nationally ranked in the top 10 in 2004, 2005, and 2006. Weintraub also coached baseball at Presbyterian College, Brevard College, and the University of Virginia. Each of these programs was nationally ranked or set a school record for wins while Weintraub was there. Brevard College did both when they went 46-10 in 1996. Additionally, Weintraub coached several select high school and collegiate summer teams.

Weintraub lives in the Dallas, TX area with his wife, Nicole, and their four children. If you have feedback on this book or would like more information about Weintraub's coaching services, public events, or speaking availability, contact him at aaron@CoachTraub.com or visit his website: www.CoachTraub.com. You can also connect with him on Facebook at Coach Traub's Mental Skills Training or *Leadership Training for Softball* and Twitter @coachtraub.